ISBN 978-1-5285-6972-9
PIBN 10081077

This book is a reproduction of an important historical work. Forgotten Books uses state-of-the-art technology to digitally reconstruct the work, preserving the original format whilst repairing imperfections present in the aged copy. In rare cases, an imperfection in the original, such as a blemish or missing page, may be replicated in our edition. We do, however, repair the vast majority of imperfections successfully; any imperfections that remain are intentionally left to preserve the state of such historical works.

# *What Makes a Nation Great*

By

## FREDERICK LYNCH, D.D.

*Secretary Federal Council Commission on Peace and Arbitration and Author of "The Peace Problem," "The New Opportunities of the Ministry," etc.*

New York    Chicago    Toronto

## Fleming  H.  Revell  Company

London    and    Edinburgh

New York: 158 Fifth Avenue
Chicago: 125 North Wabash Ave.
Toronto: 25 Richmond Street, W.
London: 21 Paternoster Square
Edinburgh: 100 Princes Street

*Dedicated to my esteemed friend*
## Edwin D. Mead
*who, for many years, has unceasingly and untiringly urged upon his country those ideals which make a nation truly great*

# CONTENTS

I. That Nation Is Greatest Which Does Most For Its People . . . 9

II. That Nation Is Greatest Which Gives the World Greatest Men . . 16

III. That Nation Is Greatest Which Teaches the World Some Great Truth . . . . . . 23

IV. That Nation Is Greatest Which Dares Trust In Justice Rather Than In Force . . . . . . . . . 32

V. That Nation Will Be Greatest Which First Practises the New Patriotism 41

VI. That Nation Will Be Greatest Which Leads the Other Nations Into the New Order . . . . . 56

VII. That Nation Is Greatest Which Practises Hospitality . . . . 69

VIII. That Nation Will Be Greatest In This Twentieth Century Which First Learns Stewardship . . . . . 79

IX. That Nation Is Greatest Which First Practises Real Democracy . . 92

X. Some Indications That the United States Is a Great Nation . . 100

**I**

## THAT NATION IS GREATEST WHICH DOES MOST FOR ITS PEOPLE

SOME time ago we listened to a distinguished American lecturing to an audience of young men on the greatness of the United States. In the course of his address he spoke somewhat as follows: We are the greatest nation in the world. We have more miles of railroad than any other country. We build the longest bridges and the highest houses. We raise more wheat than any land, and our mines of coal and ore are inexhaustible. We carry on the biggest business and produce the richest men. We eat more beef than any other people. We build the biggest battle-ships and man them with the best men. We are digging the biggest canal in the world and soon we shall have ten of the biggest cities in existence!

The writer came away from that lecture revolving many things in his mind, and chiefly this question: What makes a nation great? Is it any of these things? Have not

the greatest nations of the world—those
which all men acknowledge greatest—pos-
sessed few or none of these things? Could
not a nation to-day be great without any of
these things? Is not the United States great
just to the degree that she possesses certain
qualities which were not mentioned in this
category? Would she be great if she had
all of these things and had no character, no
fine idealism, no sense of honour, no justice
'thin her borders, no spirit of mission, no
great men, no lofty destiny in view? What are
the things that will make all the world call her
admirable, wonderful, inimitable? Is it not
*soul* rather than things that makes nations as
well as men great? This little book is the
writer's answer to these questions.

What makes a nation great? No one
would think for a moment of calling Russia
a great nation. She has illimitable stretches
of territory. No one knows what wealth of
minerals lies beneath those vast areas of
Siberian ice. She has interminable railroads.
She has wide fields of grain. She has a huge
army and is constantly increasing it. Many
of her nobles are very rich. She has even
given the world some remarkable literature
and some unique music. But with all these
things, no one names her among the great

nations.    Why?    *Because she does so little
for her people.*    She gives but scanty education to her great masses.    She bears not
their continual poverty and suffering upon
her heart.    She represses them with her iron
rule and Cossack army.    She persecutes
whole cities of her adopted sons.    She with-
holds that freedom of thought and action
which would bring them both joy in life and
splendid manhood.    She imprisons and
exiles with no trial and no mercy.    She
shows no love of a father for his children.
The government is an oppressor, not a protector.

On the other hand, there is a little nation
in the heart of Europe which would be lost
should one put it in the centre of Russia.
She has little wealth of coal and ore.    She
has no army to speak of, and no navy.    She
has no great prairies of waving grain,
although there are some fields of blue and
golden flowers.    Her chief possessions are
rock and ice.    Her only high buildings are
high because built on tops of mountains.
And yet everybody calls Switzerland a remarkable nation.    Why?    *Because she does
so much for her people.*    Every child is given
as fine an education by the state as he wants,
or, at least, needs.    Children have rights

assured them, and are never dependent upon the caprice of charity. The government is continually devising new methods of giving the child both a happy childhood and one which prepares him for manhood. One hears little of child-labour and sees no children begging. The marriage and divorce laws are framed with the happiness and welfare of the children in view. This care also extends to the whole people. Taxation is assessed to take the burden off the man using his land productively and off the poor. Every poor mother is entitled to free care in the best of maternity hospitals—and the hospital service is splendid. The state gives free burial to all. Wood is free in many cantons and the government does all it can for its people.[1]

The United States will be a great nation just in the proportion that *she cares for her people*. If she sees that every child within her border has the education he needs to grapple with the forces of nature, earn a living wage, play his part as a useful citizen, enjoy the leisure hours of day and night, rear a family decently when manhood comes, assume his share of government intelligently, and have such character as education

---

[1] See " Lessons from Switzerland," by Helen Haliburton in *Public Opinion* for January, 1913.

can give, then she will be great, though all her skyscrapers were demolished. If she sees that her children have the formative years of childhood for free and happy play, as God intended they should have, and prohibits any labour that robs them of green fields and sunlight, and forbids their employment in deep mines, and stifling mills, and overheated factories from dark of morning till dark of night, under conditions that dwarf both soul and body, then she will be great, regardless of her railroads.

If the nation becomes the great father of its people and sees that every man has economic justice, that every man who would work has opportunity to do so, that every man has a living wage, and rest and leisure to cultivate his soul, and can institute that cooperation between employer and employee that shall do away with injustice by the one and shirking of labour by the other, then it will be truly great. If she can take these vast numbers of men who come to us from lands where government means oppression, and work means exploitation and life means meagreness and drudgery, and be to them their protector from the spoiler and politician, making them learn to love her as the great father of all within her borders, then shall

she be great, indeed—greatest of all nations.
If she can provide old-age pensions for those
who, in the stress of life, can save but little,
and provide insurance against accident and
death, and take money the great empires are
piling up in armaments, which in turn become as burdensome as the first taxation,
and put this money into abolishing disease
and educating her people in health, and in-
sists on decent homes for her citizens, then
her children will love her, and other nations
will call her glorious. If she can provide
technical schools, and all sorts of institutes,
night schools and colleges, libraries, art
galleries, museums, parks, music, and play-
grounds for the little children, all this will
add to her greatness.

No. It is not mines, railroads, bridges,
beef-eating, navies, skyscrapers, telephones
that make a nation great, but the devotion
she bestows upon her children. Or, to put it
in the words of Dr. John Clifford, that nation
is great which can answer this question in
the affirmative: "Is your social order just?
What sort of character are you building?
Are you creating a happy, healthy society?
Are your ideals justice, freedom, equality of
opportunity, mutual helpfulness and universal happiness? Is your nation going as a

Good Shepherd before the sheep, restoring those who are out of the way, and carrying in its capacious bosom the lambs of the flock? Are you daring to give full sovereignty to love and good-will, sympathy to the weak and erring, help to the handicapped and restoration to the lost? Do you grow pluck and fortitude, energy of thought, alertness of mind, strength of will, magnanimity of spirit, patience under rebuffs, refusal to surrender to defeat in a good cause, and persistence against overwhelming odds? Are you bold enough to be a Christian State?

That is the question. Not, is your trade prosperous beyond precedent, or your army and navy larger than ever; but what sort of character are you developing as a people?

## II

## THAT NATION IS GREATEST WHICH GIVES THE WORLD GREATEST MEN

WHAT makes a nation great? No one ever thinks of China as a great nation. We may some day, for the huge, sleeping mass is stirring, and new impulses are at work within her breast, and a vision is dawning in her eyes. But no teacher would point out China to his boys and say: "Here is one of the leading nations of the earth; here is the ideal of progress; here is a great civilization." And why? China has unending miles of fertile plains, on which grow vast fields of rice. Her natural resources will be fabulous when our Western industry opens the gates of her locked mines. Railroads will soon run in every direction. And yet even though her material prosperity should suddenly multiply to be commensurate with her vastness, she would not be great. *She has never given the world great men.* The average man knows the name of only one great Chinaman—Confucius. Neither has she given the world a type of humanity so great that all nations point to it and say: " This is humanity worth striving for ! "

On the other hand there is a little country lying in the northern seas which has no fabulous wealth in mines or quarries; which is not big enough to have any long railroads ; which grows more heather on its barren mountains than grain ; which has no towering buildings and only one or two great bridges ; which thinks more of its universities than it does of its insurance towers ; and yet it is a country which is synonymous with greatness wherever its name is mentioned. Of course Scotland is the country to which I refer.   And why is Scotland everywhere and always great?  *Because she has given to the world great men.*  She has literally blessed the world with them.   Every generation she has produced several, and every spot on earth knows them ; even Africa, whose portals were flung open by her great son, Livingstone.   How the names roll off one's pen,— Wallace, Bruce, Knox, Montrose, of the early days, through a long list down to Burns, Scott, Carlyle, Livingstone, Chalmers, Guthrie, MacLeod, Hume, Blakie, Caird, Robertson Smith, Stevenson, Barrie, Ian Maclaren, Balfour, Bryce, Campbell-Banner-

man, John S. Kennedy, Andrew Carnegie—
one could continue the list indefinitely, from
every rank, calling and vocation.   A proces-
sion of great men carrying the genius of
Scotland into the life of every nation.   But
even more than this, Scotland has given to
the world a great race of men.   The Scotch
manhood is recognized everywhere as a high
type.   It is known for its high average in-
telligence, its mental grasp, its independent
thinking, its masterfulness of situations, its
capacity for culture, its sturdiness, its philo-
sophical   insight,   its   religious   intensity.
Scotland is great *because she has produced
great manhood*, and   who   worries   much
whether she has any Woolworth Buildings
or not?

The United States will be a great nation in
the eyes of the world just in proportion as she
continues to give the world great men.   If
she can go on producing such men as Adams,
Franklin, Washington, Jefferson, Webster,
Parker, Channing, Bushnell, Phillips, Lincoln, Whittier, Emerson, Beecher, Lowell,—
not to mention many others and omitting
living men—she will surely be counted a
great nation.   If she fail here, none of these
other things will make her noted among
men.   One needs only to bring to mind

those nations of the past, which still live in the mind of to-day, to see that they are remembered primarily for their prophets, poets, statesmen and great leaders, not for their resource, not primarily for their achievement in war or commerce. It is here that some are questioning the real greatness of our country. It was only yesterday that a London paper was giving reasons why the United States was producing no great geniuses. If we are not, it is because we are too engrossed in producing *things*. But *things* will not make us great, if with them and commanding them there are not men. The writer is not so sure that we are not on the way to give the world more great, good men. No one knows what lies dormant in the minds of these million boys, with blood of many nations coursing through their veins. It is for the nation to foster these minds to greatness if she would shine before the world.

But there is something better than giving the world great men, and that is the producing of a lofty type of manhood. Perhaps in the age of full democracy, on whose threshold we now are standing, the aim of civilization will not be so much the giving birth to a few wonderful, outstanding, giant-like heroes as the producing of a high, fearless, intelligent average humanity. The world will always need leaders, but perhaps the genius of democracy is to lift the race up on to the high table-lands, more than to generate men who stand like mountains rising out of the low valleys. Perhaps we shall develop a nation of men who can think and reason and act and see for themselves the visions they will fulfill. However that may be, that nation will be greatest in the twentieth century which produces within its borders a free and ideal humanity. What shall make our own nation great in the eyes of all the nations? Not her wealth,—not her bridges and towering structures, but the manhood of her people.

If the United States can produce the highest type of manhood the world has yet seen— a manhood that fears nothing except baseness, dares face great issues and solve them, can think for itself, has a high sense of honor, is vigorous in its intellect and clean in its heart, has strength of limb and beauty of soul, creates art and enjoys what it has created, practices justice towards all men and nations, puts the world of the spirit above the lust of material things, then all the world will point to America and say: "There is a manhood such as the world has not yet seen

—great, wonderful, star-crowned, admirable! Let us pattern after it and point our children to it."

Sometimes one cannot help feeling that America has just this opportunity of creating the highest type of manhood the world has ever seen. For no other nation has had the diversity of rare materials, such a solar spectrum of varying greatnesses, as has she, to combine into one pellucid manhood. For has not every nation of the world sent us of its best, and will not the American people that is to be, be a people in whom all these high qualities are blended? Sometimes one sees this manhood rising in the future—a manhood to which the varying and diversified gifts and highest qualities and differing temperaments and personalities of Scotch, Irish, English, German, French, Scandinavian, Austrian, Italian —and who knows but Jewish—have contributed something, and which will stand as the sort of consummation of all the manhoods of the ages, may be, perhaps, the manhood towards which creation has for ages been slowly moving, the crown of evolution, the final sons of God.

It is no dream, for the blending is already going on about us. The races are rapidly intermarrying in our great cities. Already there are children playing in our streets with blood of many countries in their veins. Let our nation bend all her energies through school, college, church, institutes, books, every resource, to fashion this composite manhood into the highest, and who knows but our nation may be greatest because she has produced greatest manhood!

## III

## THAT NATION IS GREATEST WHICH TEACHES THE WORLD SOME GREAT TRUTH

WHAT makes a nation great? No one would ever think of calling Turkey a great nation. There are many reasons why. But supposing she had many miles of railroads, great wealth of minerals, and acres of waving grain; in fact, any of the things the lecturer said make the United States great,—even then we could not call Turkey a great nation. Turkey has never given the world any of those great truths that lie at the basis of all civilization.

On the other hand, there are two little countries not far from Turkey, so small they are lost on any map of the world, but which are, perhaps, the two greatest nations the world has ever known. One of them consists mostly of sea-washed mountains and islands. She has no railroads, no bridges, hardly any material wealth. Yet Greece stands forever wonderful—crowned with glory!

For Greece gave the world one of those truths which underlies the whole fabric of civilization and has been inwrought into all the world's thinking, so that there is probably not a man who will read these words whose philosophy of life has not been shaped to some extent by the truth which that little, craggy country gave to the world 2,500 years ago. For Greece taught the world forever that the quest of the ideal is the one quest worthy of human beings; that the human soul is greater than whole universes of dead matter; that those ideas which underlie all that is best and highest in our life and thinking are invariable and universal and give light to all pure hearts; that the universe finds its ultimate meaning in free human spirits; that beauty is truth, and truth is always the most beautiful thing.

This idealism that came to us from Greece lies underneath all lofty thinking,—all great artistic achievement,—and has infused itself into all civilization which loves the good, the true, the beautiful, more than *things*.

But there is another country whose glory outshines even that of Greece. It has no railroads, no mines, no rich soil, no buildings, no wealth of any kind, not even any art, yet every child who ever lived in Christendom could tell us all about it, and has probably known its history better than that of his own land.  What country, with all the treasure in *things* that some have had, with all the greatness of arms and conquest in wars that some have achieved, has influenced the world or been called great in comparison with the little strip of barren soil we call Palestine?

And why is Palestine so great?  Simply because she gave, along with her great men and women, a great foundation truth on which our Christian civilization has been reared.  She taught the world that back of and running through all creation was the Eternal Goodness, and that His right name was Father; that men were the offspring of this Father, made in His image, therefore Sons of God; that all mankind was comprehended in the infinite love and purposes of God; that the world was not at the mercy of fitful fates and blind matter, but that it moved onward and upward to some divine consummation under the impulse and guidance of the indwelling spirit; that all creation groaneth and travaileth to bring forth perfect man and the final Kingdom of service, peace, and good-will among men; that the soul was the final wealth of great worth; that all the resources of heaven and earth existed to free

this soul and exalt it ; and that it was im-
mortal.

This message has made the very mental
and spiritual atmosphere in which we live.
It has determined the lives of countless millions, and shaped their whole conduct and
outlook upon life. On it our institutions
have been based and out of it has sprung
most of our literature. It has become a part
of our language and it is the one word which
to-day will be spoken where any man is talk-
ing of the common life. This is what it is to
be a great nation—to give the world such
truth as Greece and Palestine have given it.
And is not what greatness even Germany
and England have to-day really based on
the men they have reared and the truth their
prophets, philosophers, scientists and poets
have given the nations? That nation is
greatest which gives the world a truth that
makes its very social structure new.

The United States will be the greatest nation in the world, if, like Greece and Palestine in ancient days, she can in these modern
days give the world another truth that shall
be woven into the very warp and woof of its
destiny. And some of us dare venture to
believe that God has called her to speak
some such great word, just as He called

Greece to teach the ideal or Palestine to teach the righteous God seeking to make His children righteous, or Rome to teach order and organization under law. And is not this great truth just the one truth for which all the world is even now asking, praying for and seeking,—the truth of the brotherhood of man? And not the mere saying of it, and not the truth as a beautiful, desirable and distant aspiration, and not as an unattainable ideal to be always approximated, but as a possibility—a reality—an achievement, an object lesson to all other nations.

The very situation is God's voice calling America to this high destiny. Here are Germans, British, French, Austrians, Italians, Slavs, Russians by the millions. In the old countries they have never been able to live in peace. They have cherished ancient grudges, old injustices have rankled in their hearts. Each nation, even to-day, watches the other with alert and suspicious eyes. One familiar with the literature of Europe finds it full of a cynicism which doubts if brotherhood was not the ineffective and impossible dream of a Jesus who knew little of men or nations. (The Socialist literature is a striking exception to this statement.)

Perhaps no nation in Europe could do this

task even had she faith in it, for the old world peoples have not the divine conditions. It looks as if Providence had predestined America as the nation to put this crowning touch upon the evolution of human society. Our people have been brought here, with all their hatreds, animosities, rankling injustices, opposing points of view, and ingrained class distinctions. And lo! German and French children play together in the same street and instead of fighting or hating, marry each other when they grow up. But if they need not fight one another here, will not the question soon be asked in Europe: "Why need we fight each other here?"

This nation has the one opportunity of all history to teach the world how men of all nationalities can work together, play together, live together, govern themselves together, coöperate together, and serve each other regardless of any racial or national distinctions. The world does not believe this. It will have to believe it if the United States is true to its divine calling and one great opportunity. Even now, one who knows Europe well finds echoes of it everywhere. The author of these lines himself heard a distinguished German say: "How is it that in America Germans and English can dwell together as friends and brothers, while here we must be forever enemies?" And the United States is going to show Germany and England and the other nations that not only can these men dwell side by side as brothers, but she is going to answer this question: "How? Why?" It is simply that we are learning here that the things we all hold in common are infinitely more important than the things wherein we differ. They are more a part of our real selves, compose our being, make us *men*, while nationality, race, language, even colour, are only clothes covering a soul which everywhere is one and the same. Love, happiness, health, kindliness of soul, are the same in every heart and nation, and are greater than the things that divide us. Here we emphasize these and find that we who once thought ourselves different are really one.

The one great task of our nation is to further this brotherhood in every way. Spontaneously, out of the very conditions it is arising, but the nation must conceive it as its destiny to further it by every means. It should break down every barrier that keeps men apart; should stamp out every injustice that breeds class animosities; should purge itself of every corruption that hinders full democracy, and should teach every man who enters its golden gates that here all races are one. And let us remember that this is more a people's task than a government's. The people, not the government, are the nation. Let us who come here, whether we are German, French, Italian, Russian, Scandinavian, British, Jew or Slav, resolve to put all racial and national differences behind us forever.

Let us, while we love the land that gave us birth, as we love our mother, remember that in coming to America, we have married her, as it were, and started a new home, and our chief obligation is there. Let us resolve to be Americans first, and all other things second. Thus, this brotherhood will come. The world eagerly waits for it. Surely America has been called to teach it to the nations. If she can, she will be greatest among peoples. How splendidly Israel Zangwill has put this great truth in his recent drama: "The Melting Pot."

"Not understand that America is God's Crucible, the great melting pot where all the races of Europe are melting and reforming! Here you stand, good folk, think I, when I see them at Ellis Island, here you stand in your fifty groups, with your fifty languages and histories and your fifty blood hatreds and rivalries. But you won't be long like that, brothers, for these are the fires of God you've come to—these are the fires of God. A fig for your feuds and vendettas! Germans and Frenchmen, Irishmen and Englishmen, Jews and Russians—into the Crucible with you all! God is making the American."

# IV

## THAT NATION IS GREATEST WHICH DARES TRUST IN JUSTICE RATHER THAN IN FORCE

THERE are two ways of defending a nation. One is to build vast navies, line the shore with brazen guns and create a huge army, and then say to the other nations: "Touch us if you dare!" The other way is to be so just in all our dealings with men at home and nations abroad, to exercise such righteousness and good-will that no nation anywhere in the world will want to attack us either now or forever. That nation will be the greatest in the eyes of the future —perhaps a nearer future than we think— which dares take the new and latter way.

It is the coming way. For all the poets and prophets of all the nations have foretold it, and great numbers in our day are seeing it. It is the burden of the Gospel and there can be no real religion until it shall have come. For there can be no lasting Kingdom built on force and power which are temporal. It is the unseen things, good-will and justice, which are eternal.  Force and power can be overcome by force and power ; those nations which rest on swords will perish by the swords.  But nothing in heaven or earth can conquer justice and the spirit of good-will.

There are signs everywhere that the nations are sick unto death of the old way and still happier signs that they are distrusting it. The burden grows unbearable and there is no relief by forever adding to the burden, as we are doing to-day.  Germany builds two battle-ships, then Great Britain builds four; whereupon Germany builds six and Great Britain builds ten.  This is the program of all the nations, and every country basing its defense on added power is surely draining herself of life within.  All the resource that might go into the uplift of the nation is demanded by battle-ships and guns, while religion and education, happiness and plenty, lag behind.  All the vast wealth that the nations might use in victorious conflict against the common foe,—vice, intemperance, poverty, disease, ignorance—is expended in self-defense against fancied invaders.

And the pity of it is that force does not bring that very security each nation seeks. With millions put into armaments during the past ten years, Great Britain and Germany

dread each other more to-day than ever, and
one of these nations has been on such a verge
of panic twice during this period that she
fairly trembled. For three thousand years
now we have been basing our civilization on
force—and it has failed. We have had wars
and strifes unending and if history has any
one lesson it is that national security based
on force is an eternal fallacy and that the true
greatness of a nation has come from its exercise of righteousness—not of arms.

The great nation of the future will be
the one which dares trust in justice for security, rather than in force. Might we dare hope
that the United States will claim this high,
prophetic place and go down through all the
wonderful history that is to be, as the first nation that dared trust God, and man and justice, and be the first nation to win for herself
the title of *the great deliverer?* Perhaps it
is too much to hope, but we believe with all
our heart that should she take this high place
of leadership, she would be more secure than
the vastest navy could ever make her.

We believe that no nation would ever
think of harming her, and that her word
would carry more weight with the other nations than the word of the greatest armed
power. We believe that if this nation would

say to the world that she purposed to give justice to every man within her border and to every nation in the world, and would rest in that, she need have no force greater than that moderate police force needed to parole the seas. We believe that William Jennings Bryan was right when he made this truly Christian utterance at Lake Mohonk: "If this nation announced to the world that it would not spend its money getting ready for wars that ought never to come, that it would rather try to prevent the coming of war, that, as it did not intend to go out as a burglar, it would not equip itself with burglary tools, that it had faith in the good intent of other people, and it expected other people to have faith in its good intent, do you think our nation would suffer for that?"

Should this nation convince the world that it was "more afraid of wronging than being wronged" to use the fine words of Socrates, it would soon have the good-will of all peoples. We believe that if the people of the United States could learn "to love justice and hate wrong-doing; to be considerate in their judgment and kindly in feeling towards aliens as towards their own friends and neighbours; and to desire that their own country shall regard the rights of others rather than be grasping and overreaching," to use the words of Elihu Root, this nation would have little to fear from wars. We believe that Lord Brougham spoke the truth when he said: " Let the soldier be abroad if he will, he can do nothing in this age. There is another personage,—a personage less imposing in the eyes of some ; the schoolmaster is abroad, and I trust to him, armed with the primer, against the soldier in full military array."

We are not urging disarmament here, although the author would fear nothing for his country should she quite disarm and at the same time practice justice and good-will towards all. But granted that some armament is necessary as some police force is necessary within a city, the question is: Shall America follow in the footsteps of the old world, and becoming a great military power, as many are urging her to become, put her trust in awe-inspiring and ever increasing force, or shall she be greatest of nations and put her trust in the good-will towards her of all people, because she practiced justice and good-will first towards them ? Josephine Shaw Lowell was safer among the roughest men of the great city than the man with pistols in his hands, because she was there to do them good.

We know that many will doubt the influence and security of our country among the nations, armed with justice rather than with power, but let them remember this outstanding fact: that both her influence and her security have never depended upon her power, but upon just these moral qualities. *It has actually been her justice and not her arms* that has made her heeded of the world! When the Boxer trouble occurred in China, it was in our nation that China put her trust and confidence, and it was our words she heeded above the great armed powers. When the President of the United States intervened between warring Japan and Russia, both nations heeded us, not because of any army or navy, but because they believed that we loved justice and were disinterested people.

It is admitted by all that at the Second Hague Conference the United States carried most weight and that every nation listened when she spoke. But it was not because of a big stick behind our words. It was because the nations trusted and respected us. It is to the United States that the South American nations turn in any trouble—and would turn oftener were we more just—not because of our armament, but because they

believe in us. The formation of the Pan-
American Union in Washington and the
building of the palace by Mr. Carnegie,
which is its home, gave the United States
more influence in South America than twenty
new battle-ships would have done. Indeed,
these states never began to distrust us until
we used force and began to talk of big
navies. The United States was just as
much a world power before she had a great
navy as she is to-day.

When it comes to national security the
story is the same. If some one says that
only great force, not justice, can prevent her
being attacked and invaded by other nations, the convincing answer is : " The facts
are all against you." For one hundred years
now there has been neither fort nor battle-
ship on the three-thousand mile boundary
line between Canada and the United States,
and the people along that line to-day rest in
greater sense of security than the people
underneath the walls of Fortress Monroe.
Canada does not attack the United States
for the two simple reasons that she knows
we have nothing but good-will for her and
she has nothing but good-will for us.

But other nations ! Well, what reason is
there for any other nation having more

enmity towards us than has Canada ? Germany has none. Eight million Germans are in America and all over Germany there is affection for us because we have treated Germans as Americans,—indeed, have adopted them. To speak of arming ourselves against England is too base a thought to dwell upon, for the two nations are celebrating their one hundred years of peace. China and Japan ? We have already armed ourselves against them by disarming them of any suspicions against us. China is sending five hundred students a year to us as her invasion, and Japan is sending her lasting gratitude every day, and her admiration of our moral greatness in all dealings with her by every messenger and message.

It is our *justice* that makes us great with the nations, and not our gunboats. When our gunboats go around the world there is no evidence of the fleet increasing our greatness with the nations, and the fleet *scared no nation* as our bellicose President intended it should, simply because every nation felt it had nothing to be afraid of from the *people* of the United States. It is our justice to the foreigners who come to us, our friendliness to other countries, the belief of other nations that we have no desire or intention to seize

their land, our reputation for loving peace
rather than war, our continued advocacy of
the substitution of judicial methods for war,
that gives us power with other nations and
gives us security from attack by them.

The great mystery of our time is that so
many cannot see facts so patent, and go on
clamouring for the United States to fall back
into the littleness and transiency of those
who trust in force, when she ought to be
moving first of all out into the greatness of
those who trust in national character. For
*character* is going to be both the power and
safeguard of the great nations of the future
as it long has been the power and security
of all great men. It was said of David
Livingstone that his *goodness* made him
secure against all attacks from savages.
But to-day nations are civilized, and surely
our goodness would save us from them all.
If one nation is the first to see this, she is
going to be the greatest nation the earth has
ever known.

## V

## THAT NATION WILL BE GREATEST WHICH FIRST PRACTISES THE NEW PATRIOTISM

THE earliest form of patriotism consisted in the hatred of all other countries but one's own. It manifested itself in frequent wars, and he was the greatest patriot who had slain the most men of other nations. It has not altogether vanished from the earth, although it is not the prevalent manifestation in our day. It was only fifteen years ago that a Frenchman remarked that the chief patriotic sentiment he had had drilled into him as a child was hatred of Germany. There have been attempts to revive it in Germany and England ; fierce bigots have tried to stir up hatred in each of these nations against the other, but with only partial success. It has largely perished in the United States, and recent attempts to " kindle patriotism " by influencing hatred towards Japan and towards England have proved most abortive. We have passed beyond that stage. The average

American no longer conceives hatred of the foreigner as equivalent to love of his own country.

But if we have passed beyond this crude and somewhat barbaric form of patriotism, there is still much left of a phase of it that is both mischievous and unworthy of men who would see their nation truly great. This consists of a blind devotion to one's nation, regardless of her course, and is expressed in a motto, than which one more opposed to the ultimate welfare of a nation never existed: " My country, may she be always right, but my country right or wrong," which motto would place one's country on exactly the same level with those lodges which defend their members, even when they are proven criminals.

Its latest manifestation was in Italy, where certain Italians confessed that their country did wrong in breaking the Hague covenant and in seizing Tripoli simply for territory, but, she having done so, it was their duty to stand by her. Those few who loved the fair name of Italy enough to protest, were persecuted as were those real lovers of their country who in England protested against the Boer War. Happily this ideal of patriotism is passing. At least, it is not emphasized so much in times of peace. But there is enough of it left to suddenly seize a nation when war breaks out. It was not long ago that our own people forgot to ask whether the attack on Spain was just or unjust, when the nation had been fanned into the war frenzy by the jingoes and screeching press.

The form of patriotism that is perhaps that which lies in the subconsciousness of most Americans to-day is a sort of emergency patriotism. In times of peace it consists of a somewhat sentimental devotion to one's country, exemplified mostly in saluting the flag and singing national hymns, and in times of war the willingness to die for one's country. Even to-day, patriotism in most people's minds is associated with war. The patriot is one who has died on the field of battle. The monuments are mostly built to soldiers. Our patriotic hymns gather about war. Our two patriotic occasions are Independence Day and Memorial Day. Our histories and orations have, until quite recently, praised only the soldier as patriot. We welcome under triumphal arches and with mighty acclamations those returning from the wars as our great children.

In reaction from this false and primitive patriotism it is not necessary to go to the extremes of Tolstóy or Hervè or Moscheles, although it is natural enough that these men should have come to dread the very word, seeing, as they have, how this perverted form of it has stood in the way of that growth of humanity as a whole which is greater than the fancied welfare of any nation ; and seeing as they have, how it has always emphasized a nation's rights instead of her duties (which principle, when applied to individuals, is considered unchristian by this same people). But inherently, there is no more reason why a·proper love of one's country should interfere with a devotion to humanity any more than a love of one's home should prescribe one's devotion to his native land. Where all of these writers are probably right, however, is in their contention that most love of country is a manufactured, artificial thing. Even the old-fashioned patriotism did not spring spontaneous from childlike hearts, but was an expression of passions along avenues previously prepared for it.

Their contention that most countries have never done enough for their people to elicit any natural affection is probably true in many instances. But where nations are striving to care for their people, as some are to-day, there is no reason why there should not be an affection for them, and likewise there is no reason why this affection should not assume such form as to be not only beautiful and commendable, but of genuine service to all humanity, just as a man's love for his home may be the most helpful asset of the community.

There are many signs that this "new patriotism" is rising upon the souls of men. It is running like a thread of light through much of our best literature and poetry. It is seen in the utterances of our greatest statesmen— those who feel the movements of this century and can sense their high direction. It appears in all this sudden international organization of all churches, societies and institutions, and in the innumerable world congresses being held. The remarkable spread of the peace movement in recent years is but a manifestation of it. The Hague Conferences are an outgrowth of it. The rising of the gospel of the brotherhood of man has gone on beside it. The coöperative instinct everywhere observed among the labouring men of Europe, regardless of nationality, is a pronounced flowering of it. It is a patriotism of peace, and not of war, a patriotism "whose courage is of life, not death." It is a heroism of service and not of destruction. It is love of country which, while true to the highest in one's own nation, at the same time blesses every other. It is a national devotion which is stripped of all that selfishness that makes it exclusive and provincial. It is a patriotism in which all nations will rejoice with the nation which holds it.

The nation that can first learn and practise it will be the greatest nation of the twentieth century. Will the United States be this nation? Yes, if she can convince her people that real love of country manifests itself in a passionate desire to make one's land just and honourable, and the fairest and freest of all lands. Already this newer patriotism has taken deep root in many hearts, and our most gifted leaders are realizing that true patriotism reveals itself not in shouting, singing or fighting, but in a real devotion to the country's highest welfare.

The patriotism of the twentieth century will insist that the nation treat every man within her borders justly, and see that he gets justice. And likewise it will demand that the nation keep her promise made to other nations, for it will see that her loss of honour is greater than her loss of territory, or of a few lives in battle. It would be infinitely more of a degradation to our nation to lose the respect of Europe because we broke our treaty promises than to have lost the Spanish War. This new patriotism will realize that political purity and legislative honesty are far higher assets of a nation than huge fleets and armies.

So the patriot of the future will be the man who lives for his country, as well as dies for it, and he who dies in her service while *saving* life will be a greater patriot than he who dies for her while destroying other lives. The hero of the future will be of the industrial, professional, and labouring world, not of the battle-field, except as he may defend his country from wanton attack. (The United States will never be attacked if true patriotism prevails and makes her just and honourable.) The hero fund, whose awards are always to go to those who save life, never to those who take it, is not only a premonition of the new patriotism, but has wonderfully helped its coming by directing the attention of the world from the battle-field to the civic and industrial sphere as the true field of bravery. Not insignificant is it that at a recent vote taken in the Paris schools on France's greatest hero, the vote which twenty years ago would have put Napoleon, who took over three million lives, at the head of the list, placed him far down the list, and hailed Pasteur as the true patriot of France.

Richard Watson Gilder has put the spirit of the new patriotism in lines that cannot be too often quoted:

" 'Twas said: ' When roll of drum and battle's roar
  Shall cease upon the earth, O, then no more

" ' The deed, the race, of heroes in the land.'
  But scarce that word was breathed when one small
      hand

" Lifted victorious o'er a giant wrong
  That had its victims crushed through ages long;

" Some woman set her pale and quivering face,
  Firm as a rock, against a man's disgrace;

" A little child suffered in silence lest
  His savage pain should wound a mother's breast;

" Some quiet scholar flung his gauntlet down
  And risked, in Truth's great name, the synod's
      frown;

" A civic hero, in the calm realm of laws,
  Did that which suddenly drew a world's applause;

" And one to the pest his lithe young body gave
  That he a thousand thousand lives might save."

Will the United States be the nation to first learn the new patriotism? Yes, if she can convince her people that their real enemies are not outside her borders, but within her walls, and direct their energies to fighting these imminent and threatening foes instead of expending them upon imagined enemies or in wars which leave no gain. The real enemies of the United States are not England, Germany or Japan, but the liquor interests; those who purvey vice and live on it; those who adulterate foods; those who buy up legislatures, take bribes and receive graft; those who exploit children for profit; those who conduct business on the level with pirates; those who defraud the people and the government. These are the real enemies of the United States.

No truer words have been spoken than those of one of our eminent judges: "The dangers, if any exist to the nation, the state, or the city, are not in things outside of them; not in the Yellow Peril, not in foreign enemies, nor in foreign countries. The dangers lurk deeper, in the distemper, the bad spirit, the ignorance, corruption, evasion of jury duty and other public duties, and apathy among the people, in popular errors concerning the law, the state, and our obligations to it."

The patriotism of the future will be directed to saving the nation from these real enemies, and will have no thought of the old warfare with nations in the hard fight against these foes.   It will also expend itself in making these thousands of foreigners who come to us, knowing nothing of our ways or ideals, but potential with superb good for the nation, into good citizens.  Sacrificial citizenship is the coming patriotism.  It will expend itself in creating a nation's honour, not defending it.  "Honour's wounds are always self-inflicted," says Mr. Carnegie, in one of the truest and finest epigrams ever uttered. Those who have fought disease, poverty, and vice will have the monuments of the future, —not those who have fought the Spaniards.

The new patriotism will be as intense a love of country as was the old, but it will take the form of wanting to make her as good and great as possible for the service she can render all other nations.  The patriot of the future will devote himself ardently to his country, in order that he make her such a nation as can be an example to all others ; protector of all weak countries, haven of all oppressed peoples, guardian of all threatened liberties, champion of human rights in all lands, missionary of light and knowledge, science and truth to all backward races, mother of all childlike peoples, nurse of all famine-stricken lands, leader in all high causes. Who would not love with maternal devotion the nation who strove thus to bless all peoples? How greatest among nations the United States will be, if some day she attain this high ideal.

And, best of all, the United States will be the greatest nation in the world if she can be first to teach her people the patriotism that is surely rising on the vision of the world—namely, that dedication to humanity is higher than devotion to city, state, or country alone. It is what has been called the cosmic patriotism—the feeling that man is one in all his aspirations and despairs, victories and defeats, joys and sorrows, with all men everywhere, regardless of race or nationality. It is what Mrs. Elmer Black has called " the new world-consciousness," the sense of citizenship in humanity as being greater than citizenship in any land. It is what many are calling the new internationalism,—the sense that in this twentieth century of banished distances and inter-related life, all the nations are wrapt up in the same destiny.

It does not mean that one should love his country less, any more than it means that love of country prevents one devoting himself to the welfare of his state. But it does mean the consciousness that all men are our brothers and that neighbourhood is not to be bounded by sect, race or nation, but by manhood and by need. It is the vision that Lowell caught fifty years ago when he sang that prophetic song of the true man's fatherland being wherever men were in bonds or seeking the same high freedom as himself. It is the great proclamation of the Gospel that membership in the Kingdom of God should transcend all lesser boundaries. It is the growing sense of the brotherhood of man as being the final test of all one's actions—even above citizenship in any state. When it comes it will mean the end of war, for all wars spring from devotion to state or nation being put above love of humanity or sense of human brotherhood. To a Tolstoy, participation in war is impossible, because a German or a Frenchman is as much his brother as a Russian. This will be the patriotism of us all when we begin to comprehend Jesus, for it is His fundamental teaching on its social side.

And it is coming faster than men dream. Already the working men of England, Germany and France, in their annual congresses are asking: " Why should we fight each other, simply because we are born under different flags? Are we not all men of common ambitions, common struggles, common joys?" Already the poets and preachers are seeing it, and many dramatists and chroniclers of stories. Here and there are great statesmen rising out of the provincialism of the old patriotism into the world outlook of the new. All our organizations, religious, social, economic, scientific, literary, are becoming international and are holding *world* congresses by the score. Every one of these congresses is a step towards this sense of international unity,—world citizenship.

That international hospitality or exchange of visits of eminent citizens of different countries everywhere is growing, and when the reciprocal visits of rulers shall come, for which Mr. Carnegie so beautifully appeals in his New Year's letter of 1913, it will mean that they shall " discard distrust and learn to trust each other, and the chief nations will soon begin to act in unison, drawing the others with them into International Peace."

In our own nation it is coming fast—and this makes us hope that here will come the new patriotism first, and America be greatest —because here have been thrown together all the nations of the world into one community

life, and in common, kindly, helpful, coöperative living, in friendships and intermarriages.
Scandinavians, Germans, French, Poles,
Slavs, Italians and Greeks, are learning that
those national distinctions that once made
them foes were passing accidents, while their
common humanity is the eternal and abiding
thing.

No one has more beautifully expressed this
than has Jane Addams in " Newer Ideals of
Peace" and with her prophetic words we
close this chapter: "It is possible that we
shall be saved from warfare by the 'fighting
rabble' itself, by the 'quarrelsome mob'
turned into kindly citizens of the world
through the pressure of a cosmopolitan
neighbourhood.   It is not that they are
shouting for peace—on the contrary, if they
shout at all, they will continue to shout for
war—but that they are really attaining cosmopolitan relations through daily experience.
They will probably believe for a long time
that war is noble and necessary both to
engender and cherish patriotism ; and yet all
of the time, below their shouting, they are
living in the kingdom of human kindness.
They are laying the simple and inevitable
foundations for an international order as the
foundations of tribal and national morality

have already been laid. They are developing the only sort of patriotism consistent with the intermingling of the nations; for the citizens of a cosmopolitan quarter find an insuperable difficulty when they attempt to hem in their conception of patriotism either to the 'old country' or to their adopted one.

"There arises the hope that when this newer patriotism becomes large enough, it will overlook arbitrary boundaries and soak up the notion of nationalism. We may then give up war, because we shall find it as difficult to make war upon a nation at the other side of the globe as upon our next-door neighbour.'

## VI

## THAT NATION WILL BE GREATEST WHICH LEADS THE OTHER NATIONS INTO THE NEW ORDER

A NEW order is rising in the minds of men. For three thousand years our civilization has been based on force. By far the greater part of all the money of the past has gone into war and preparation for war. The nations have spent ten dollars on militarism to every one on education. Even to-day, there is but one nation spending as much on her schools as on her armaments. The nations of Europe are groaning under war debts that perhaps they never can pay. The real rulers of Europe to-day are not her kings or her people but certain great banking houses, which have all the nations in their power.[1] Most of the inventive genius of the past has gone into implements of destruction.

Things have changed somewhat, but even to-day the chief interest in air-ships centres in their use as instruments of war. The

[1] See "The Unseen Empire," by David Starr Jordan.

nations have given their best life to war, and left the weaklings to breed the present race. The men of Europe are physically, mentally, and morally far inferior to what they might have been had not all her noblest, best and bravest been destroyed in battle, leaving the race to be bred by those unfit for war. This is the price we have paid for a civilization based on force—this in addition to the immeasurable suffering, sorrow, anguish, poverty, hatred, revenge, disease, and retarded civilization.

And the nations are not far out of this slough of despond, this swamp of misery. The burden of armament is fast becoming too great to bear. Wars are less frequent, but they still persist. In the preparation for war there is no cessation at all. Germany and England are in a mad race of battle-ship building that not only promises to bankrupt both nations soon, but is taking the millions of dollars they need to lift their people out of poverty, ignorance and disease. The other nations are following close behind. Hundreds of thousands of men are taken from productive labour every year. The genius of men is turned in the direction of force. The minds of men are continually kept upon force as the basis of civilization. Armament is so much more prominent than religion that men distrust the latter and instinctively trust in force. Guns are more in evidence than gospel, therefore men trust in guns. The burden grows more and more unbearable.

In all these lands there is a yearning among great masses to find some way out. In every nation there is a growing number of prophetic men who are beginning to catch a glimpse of a better way; who are seeing visions of a new order, based not on force but on justice; not upon guns but upon gospel; not upon battle-ship but upon statesmanship; not upon militarism but upon good-will; not upon war, but upon law; not on arming against each other, but on coöperation and brotherhood; not on violence and destruction, but on righteousness and friendly ministry.

The possibility of a court where nations can take their disputes, as states and individuals take theirs, and of arbitration treaties binding nations to the same agreements that now bind all gentlemen in their relationships, is becoming a sure and fixed conviction in more minds every year. In every nation, men are believing that a body of law can be made by the nations for all the nations, which it shall be criminal to break. A greater unity of the world is being hailed in every land. The new order of law and statesmanship, good-will and international unity, is surely possible, and as inevitable some day as is freedom from despotism. That will be the greatest nation which can lead the other nations up into these shining table-lands.

The United States should be the one nation to achieve this greatness of leading all the other governments into the new order where international relationships shall be based on law and justice, as individual and national relationships already are. Everything designates her as the prophet and leader of this certain evolution. Her position makes it easy for her. With two great oceans, worth whole areas of fleets and lines of forts, she need take little thought of self-defense. She has no entangling alliances with other nations, no enemies among them, no ancient feuds and jealousies between herself and other powers; she is esteemed of all, and until recently was believed of all nations to be seeking justice above self-interest. When she has spoken, the other nations have listened, and because of this aloofness from the strife and mutual jealousies of European states, her words have carried weight.

The constitution of her population gives
her supreme right to speak the leading word
in common friendliness and good-will, because she has proved its possibility within
her own borders where all the ancient warring nations are now living in kindly, mutual relationship. Andrew Carnegie has well
said: "Well do the intelligent masses of
Europe and of our southern republics know
and appreciate the mission of this Republic
in drawing all ranks and classes together in
the bonds of brotherhood. Her representa-
tives will not lack support in these lands or
in Canada when they urge that all international disputes shall be arbitrated that the
world's peace may remain unbroken."

The United States has led in this movement from the beginning. Our great statesmen, William Penn, Benjamin Franklin,
George Washington, Thomas Jefferson,
Charles Sumner, William Lloyd Garrison,
Abraham Lincoln, Ulysses S. Grant, John
Hay, David J. Brewer, and nearly all the
others to Elihu Root, William J. Bryan,
William H. Taft, and Woodrow Wilson
have been ardent advocates of the new order,
—the substitution of courts and treaties for
wars and armament. Our greatest prophets
have lifted up their voices or penned their

burning words against war and in favour of law and justice.

The American Church may well be proud that, almost without exception, her great prophets have spoken passionately on this theme,—such preachers as Bushnell, Channing, Beecher, Hale, Brooks, and Bradford. And to-day—let us record it here—there is hardly a minister of any eminence in the whole nation who is not eloquently pleading for the United States to lead the world into the new order. All our poets have been singers of the new day, and our literature is rich in peace poems from the pens of Emerson, Lowell, Longfellow and Whittier.

America has always had a splendid group of men who have organized associations for the promotion of international arbitration— William Ladd, Elihu Burritt, William Dodge, Albert K. Smiley, Benjamin F. Trueblood, Alfred Love, Edwin D. Mead, and many others. It is in our land that the business men have turned idealists and have offered their voice and money to make the United States the leader of nations—such men as Andrew Carnegie and Edwin Ginn. The educators, headed by such college presidents as Nicholas Murray Butler, Charles W. Eliot, and David Starr Jordan, have made the peace movement part of their life-work, and have contributed much to its swift advancement.

The United States has played an important part in the two Hague Conferences. At the Second Hague Conference she it was who initiated and pressed the leading measures either discussed or adopted, such as the permanent court of nations, arbitration treaties, prize courts and the abolition of the collecting of private debts by nations. Her record has been great and honourable and she has easily been foremost among nations in urging the reign of law.

And now is she to renounce her high and unique leadership, sacrifice her chance of greatness and let England or France take her place? There was no sign of it previous to these recent years; indeed, three years ago it looked as though she were going to crown her leadership with a great act that would sound the death knell of war. The then President of the United States sent a thrill of exultation through the heart of the nation by saying that he believed the time had come when nations ought to agree to settle *all* their disputes, of whatever character, by arbitration.

It was a proud moment for the United States, for it was her President who was the first ruler of a great nation to take this prophetic stand. Mr. Taft followed up his epoch making utterance with a still greater step. He proposed that this nation offer Great Britain and France such general treaties of arbitration as he had advocated. Great Britain and France not only signified their willingness to accept these treaties, but went so far as to affix their signatures to them. And then our nation took its first backward step ; for the first time in history renounced its high leadership. The United States Senate (let us acknowledge by closest vote) refused to ratify these treaties as framed by the President and the Department of State, and so emasculated them as to make them little better than those partial treaties all nations have been making for years. It was the great national renunciation. The nation missed her supreme chance of greatness. She will never be truly great until she repents of this act and offers to sign these unlimited compacts with Great Britain, France, Germany and Japan.

Meantime, with the election of Woodrow Wilson to the Presidency of the United States and William Jennings Bryan to be Secretary of State, the United States has been given an opportunity to redeem itself and make reparation for its betrayal of the people. For we believe the Senate in refusing to ratify the treaties with Great Britain and France acted contrary to the desires of the people. Hardly had they rejected the proposals of Mr. Taft when President Wilson and Mr. Bryan came forward with new treaty proposals, which, while not so absolute and sweeping in their terms, yet would, if adopted, probably accomplish, in time, the same end, namely, the substitution of judicial procedure for war in the settlement of all disputes between our country and other nations.

The treaties, as proposed by Mr. Bryan, provide that in case a dispute should arise between the United States and any other nation, the two countries shall refrain from going to war until an International Commission has given the whole subject most careful consideration and investigation, to see if the dispute cannot be settled by judicial procedure, rather than by war. This committee is to have a year in which to make its report and neither nation is bound to abide by it.

These proposals mark such an advanced step in international peace that they deserve most careful reading. They are as follows:

" ARTICLE I. The high contracting parties agree that all disputes between them, of every nature whatsoever, which diplomacy shall fail to adjust, shall be submitted for investigation and report to an International Commission, to be constituted in a manner prescribed in next succeeding article; and they agree not to declare war or to begin hostilities during such investigation or report.

"ARTICLE II. The International Commission shall be composed of five members, to be appointed as follows:

"One member shall be chosen from each country by the Government thereof, one member shall be chosen by each Government from some third country, the fifth member shall be chosen by common agreement between the two Governments. The expenses of the commission shall be paid by the two Governments in equal proportion.

"The International Commission shall be appointed within four months after the exchange of the ratification of this treaty, and vacancies shall be filled according to the manner of the original appointment.

"ARTICLE III. In case the high contracting parties shall have failed to adjust a dispute by diplomatic methods, they shall at once refer it to the International Commission for investigation and report. The International Commission may, however, act upon its own initiative, and in such cases it shall notify both Governments and request their coöperation in their investigation.

"The report of the International Commission shall be completed within one year after the date on which it shall declare its investigation to have begun, unless the high contracting parties shall extend the time by mutual agreement. The report shall be prepared in triplicate: one copy shall be presented to each Government and the third retained by the commission for its files.

"The high contracting parties reserve the right to act independently on the subject matter of the dispute after the report of the commission shall have been submitted.

"ARTICLE IV. Pending the investigation and report of the International Commission, the high contracting parties agree not to increase their military or naval programmes, unless danger from a third power should compel such increase. In which case, the party feeling itself menaced shall confidentially communicate the fact in writing to the other contracting party, whereupon the latter shall also be released from its obligation to maintain its military and naval status quo.

" ARTICLE V. The present treaty shall be ratified by the (here names of the officials who have the power to sign and ratify treaties in the various nations will be entered), and by the President of the United States of America, by and with the advice and consent of the Senate thereof, and the ratifications shall be exchanged as soon as possible. It shall take effect immediately after the exchange of ratifications, and shall continue in force for a period of five years; and it shall thereafter remain in force until twelve months after one of the high contracting parties has given notice to the other of an intention to terminate it."

The proposals have already met with gratifying response from the different nations. President Wilson and Secretary Bryan have confidence—on what grounds we know not—that the Senate will ratify the treaties as they may be signed. They are not as satisfactory as Mr. Taft's original propositions, which bound the nation to arbitrate its disputes unless an international commission declared the dispute non-justiciable. There remains the *possibility* of war. But there remains no *probability* of war. As a matter of fact, all students of world politics feel, with Secretary Bryan, that when two nations found themselves on the verge of a quarrel, should they refrain for one year, calmly awaiting a report of an impartial commission, which would certainly report the dispute capable of arbitration, their passions would so cool off that they would have no desire to fight each other. It is only when passions are kindled that either men or nations desire war. Let them wait a year, refraining from preparation for war, maintaining friendly relations while the commission was carrying on its investigations and risk of war would pass away.

Again our country has stepped to the front in the leadership for greatness. Let us hope that before Mr. Wilson and Mr. Bryan pass out of office, the United States will have signed these treaties with every nation of the globe.

# VII

## THAT NATION IS GREATEST WHICH PRACTISES HOSPITALITY

A NATION'S growth to greatness follows, to a marked degree, the same laws as those which make man great. The great man is he who contributes most to the world of truth, or invention, or art, or organization, or blessing of any sort. The great nation is that which contributes most to civilization. The great man is he who is honourable, charitable, clean, heroic, of lofty ideal. The great nation practises justice and stands in honour before the world. The great man is he who rights wrongs, stamps out injustices, befriends the weak. Surely, this is the test of greatness we are now applying to nations. But beyond this the great man is always the hospitable man. He has kept his mind open to new truth, new ideas, new visions dawning on the world. He has kept in close touch with humanity and enriched his own life from contact with other souls. He has eschewed provinciality and generally has gone far beyond national-

ity in the enrichment of his life, seeking the
gifts of art, literature, ideas, ideals, and religion from every land.  It is this that makes
large, rich, great manhood.  It is this that
will also make a nation great.

This truth is now so strikingly in process
of illustration before our very eyes that it
hardly needs further emphasis.  Sometimes
it looks as if Japan's rapid stride towards
greatness began on the day she offered hospitality to outside truth, ideals, and whatever
has worth.  It is not quite fair, however, to
say that her greatness began at that moment,
because she had already begun to evince
greatness when she decided to invite the
Western culture in.  But the real greatness
of Japan has been due largely to her hospitality, which has been more marked than in
almost any other nation.

As a consequence her greatness has developed faster.  She has thrown her doors
wide  open, and has freely invited in all the
Christian religion has to give, and has not
only adopted it widely, but where she has
not openly done so, has let its ideals per-
meate all her institutions and contribute what
they  may  to existing religions.  She has invited  in the Western education, all its books
and  methods, and  then framed an excellent

system of her own.  She has invited in all the science of the world and used it freely in her industrial development and in her warfare against disease.  She imported Western machinery by daily boat loads and began to grow rich.  She sought our culture, importing our books by the thousands, and even sending thousands of students yearly to the colleges of America and Europe.

She freely used those principles of constitutional government that have been found successful in other nations when she wished to democratize her own government.  It has been the most pronounced instance of lavishly exercised hospitality the world has seen.  It has been perhaps the most phenomenal exhibition of speedily acquired greatness the world has known.  And now China is opening her doors, and she is feeling the pulse of life, and she too will go on towards greatness, if she can practise hospitality.

We are sure that when the history of America's surprising growth into real greatness during the last century comes to be written, it will be said: "Her hospitality has made her great."  A hundred years ago she opened her doors to all peoples; she invited all the races of the earth to come and be her guests.  She even erected a great statue at her gates to give them welcome as they came. She has offered them citizenship on easiest terms compatible with safety, and she has freely educated them in the schools.

To-day she is great because of that hospitality. For all the nations, acting on her hospitality, came with their best. England, Scotland and Ireland sent their sturdiest and brightest to us. From Scandinavia came the youngest and best. Eight millions of Germans have come with their genius for thoroughness. The Italian has come with his strong arms to dig and his instinct for song and colour. While from all those lands south and east of Austria have come a great multitude of clean limbed, vigorous young workers who are making the wealth of America in mines, factories and shops.

And it is the best that have responded to her hospitality. It is the ambitious man, the young man with dreams and with courage to fulfill them who leaves Croatia, crosses Europe and follows the broad Atlantic to our shores. We have become great from those whom their fatherlands would gladly have kept at home.

It is the greatest mistake in the world to think that it is the scum of the earth that comes to America. It is the strongest, sturdiest, most healthful, most aspiring. They have come and they have helped make America. They have built her railroads, tunnelled her mountains, mined her coal and ore, erected her great cities, tilled her illimitable soil; and the second and third generations have become her business men and artisans, her professional men and teachers, holders of office, and members of legislatures. They are America's real wealth. It is they who have helped make her great. What art and music she has yet produced has been largely brought by them. And when one names our great men, how many of them are ours not by birth but by hospitality—such names as Carl Schurz, Theodore Thomas, Leopold Damrosch, John S. Kennedy, Andrew Carnegie, William S. Rainsford, Frank Kneisel, Robert Collyer, Anton Seidl, John Hall, and William M. Taylor.

These are only a few. How much poorer America would have been to-day had she closed her gates after 1812 and kept them shut; how much more provincial. Her hospitality brought these millions, all with their best contributions, and America has comprehended these varied characteristics of all nations and they have made her great. And she shall be greater still.

The man who is hospitable to truth and ideals from whatever source is the man who grows. The man who keeps open heart and mind, not the man who hedges himself about with walls and fences, is the man who grows great in culture, resource, and strength. The same is true of nations. Here is the danger of tariffs. Apart from any political considerations, granting that occasionally it may be necessary to protect an infant industry for a while, yet fundamentally the whole system of barring out good things is the one policy contradictory to greatness. Particularly is this true when a nation would bar out works of art, books, and science. It is these things that minister to greatness.

Our smallness at present is most conspicuous here. We have not produced much great art, and no great music. While we have contributed much to natural science and practical invention, yet how poor we should be if we depended on America alone for our great books! It is from Germany that Kant, Hegel, Spinoza, Fichte, Schleiermacher, Goethe, Schiller, Lessing, Richter, Heine, Eucken, Harnack, Haeckel—a hundred more—come to us. It is from England and Scotland that Chaucer, Shakespeare, Milton, Burns, Darwin, Spencer, Wordsworth,

Coleridge, Lamb, Shelley, Keats, Tennyson, Browning, Ruskin, and Matthew Arnold come to us—from them that we must invite the great philosophers and scientists of the eighteenth and nineteenth century. How poverty stricken our intellectual and artistic life would have been had we not been hospitable! Let us never dream of doing anything to exclude these things. Our greatness lies in removing every restriction and freely and even beseechingly inviting all art, music, science, books to our shores.

This century is going to put our nation to the test again along these very lines of hospitality. Certain new ideals of human relationship of the social order and of what we call ..iotism are rising, if as yet somewhat va. .iy and incoherently, in every land. M. .ing allowance for the crude forms in which these ideals may at times shape themselves politically and socially, granting that they occasionally emerge in exaggerated and fantastic form, yet they are the ideals that will be the reality of the next century.

Unless all the signs of all the nations, all literature, all social movements, must be absolutely discredited, these things are sure: that the next century is going to see the competitive economic order largely sup-

planted by the coöperative, going to witness
the transfer of all the expenditures of nations
from guns wherewith to kill each other to the
rooting out of disease, poverty, ignorance,
and the establishment of industries, homes,
and plenty for everybody ; going to witness
—indeed, it is already seeing it—the enlarge-
ment of patriotism from an unreasoning devotion to one country to a cosmic patriotism
whose chief loyalty is to humanity.

In substance, these are the three ideals
that are emerging from all the social unrest,
the political agitation, the literature of Europe. The echoes are already in our own
land. The platforms of the three political
parties of 1912 showed signs of it. They
are appearing in our literature. Our great
labour organizations are groping towards
them, if often blindly. They are finding
more and more emphasis in the churches,
even with somewhat formidable opposition
from those saints who are always trying to
hold back the sea. They are as inevitable
in some form or other as democracy was in
France, England and America a hundred
years ago.

That nation is going to be greatest which,
instead of fearing these ideals, welcomes
them with hospitality and leads the world in

their rational application to life. The United States will be greatest in the degree that she shows hospitality to them beyond other nations. Let us wish for her that she should not let France or Germany or even England take her crown here. The coöperative ideal in industry is making great progress in Germany and they who believe in it are growing rapidly in numbers and influence.

The feeling that militarism as the basis of the political order has had its day and that the governments must stop spending all their resources on armament, and must put it on constructive ventures, productive of human welfare and happiness, is finding a rapidly growing group of advocates in Great Britain. The insistence on a larger and cosmic patriotism is continually finding utterance in the writings of France. These ideals are going to forge ahead very rapidly. The horror and absurdity of the unspeakable Balkan orgy have convinced thousands in Europe that wars are not only foolish and sinful but futile.

Great changes in ideals are soon to sweep across the world. These three are going to arise as the old ones fall away. Our country must hurry if she would be first. She has a wonderful opportunity to lead here, because

she has so much democracy on which to
build, and these ideals are nothing but the
logical flowering of democracy.   She already
has the materials of a cosmic patriotism,
because half of her citizens call other nations
father and mother, while they have adopted
this country as their own.   Here, too, people
from every land have learned to be friendly
towards each other and to see that attach-
ments are not based on nationality but upon
humanity.   Let our nation be hospitable to
these dawning and larger conceptions of the
social economic and political order, and she
will add another mark of greatness to her
score

# VIII

## THAT NATION WILL BE GREATEST IN THE TWENTIETH CENTURY WHICH FIRST LEARNS STEWARDSHIP

THE test of national greatness in the past has always been the capacity to make all other nations bring tribute. That has been the greatest nation which could take the most from other nations, which could steal the most, conquer the most, destroy the most men or cities, subdue other nations under her feet. The practically universal praise of poets and historians has been bestowed upon the great empire building nations, and regardless of what use they made of the empire. England has been great in the eyes of the world because she seized India and other lands. All over Italy, since Italy stole Tripoli, the press has been saying : " At last Italy has awakened to a consciousness of her greatness." Practically all history has been written from this point of view—the greatest nation has been that nation which has stolen, destroyed, devastated, or, at least, subdued other nations and peoples. Rome was greatest of them all.

Curiously enough, all this we praise in nations is what we have long ago ceased praising in men. We condemn men who steal and destroy, and call them mean and vile and despicable, not great. He is the greatest man who gives the most, not gets the most; who saves life, not destroys it. Of course it has not always been so. There was a time when the greatest man was he who did just exactly what we now think great in nations; who stole, subdued, and killed the most.

The Cæsars and Napoleons and William the Conquerors used to be our greatest heroes. The men who could build up huge fortunes in our own America, regardless of any method, used to be recorded as America's greatest men. But all this has changed. The great men of to-day are not the Napoleons but the Pasteurs. We honour the men who save life,—not those who destroy it. The great man is not he who *gets* the most, but he who *gives* the most. We determine a man's genius even, not by his ability to acquire a vast fortune, but by his ability to use it where it will most forward human evolution. The great man to-day is he who renders most service to humanity; who considers himself steward of whatever trusts God may have given him; who, in his greatness, befriends the weak and helpless; whose heart is set on duties rather than on rights.

The question is whether this is not to be the test of a nation's greatness in the twentieth century. Is not that nation to be greatest which can forget its self-interest occasionally and go out; which can be the friend and helper of the weaker nations; which can demand that justice be done in the world; which can have the sense of *mission*, of being sent to seek not its own only, but to bless others; which can learn that it is giving which makes a nation great, as it is giving and serving which makes men noble? There are already signs of a tendency to bring nations up to the same test as that which we now apply to men.

There was a condemnation of Italy's high-handed action in Tripoli in the press of Europe and America that would have been unknown twenty years ago. There is a wide-spread feeling, seen in Europe and America, that the time for the exploitation of weaker nations by powerful ones has gone by. The recognition of the right of any big nation to seize any little one it wanted to would not be so easily obtained to-day as a quarter of a century ago.

There was in England a large and powerful group which protested against England entering upon the Boer War, declaring that she was sacrificing her honour and true greatness. All over the world a new literature is being born, with this as its key-note.

But how is it with our own country? Is she leading in this regard? Is she "going out" more than any other nation, to befriend and bless—to serve and develop other lands? Is she learning to put aside that national greed and stealing, which, until very recently, even our churches have praised and blessed, and even sink her own rights for the sake of lifting other nations up and securing welfare for them? Perhaps this is to be the ultimate test of national greatness in the twentieth century as it is already the final test of human nobleness. Let us be glad that we can say, up to the present time, that the United States has led in this high test of greatness.

The signs of this are the things of which our nation should be proudest. We forgot our greatness; yielded to the frenzy of the jingoes and yellow journals and plunged into an absolutely unnecessary war with Spain. But it is to the nation's lasting credit that she has treated the lands accidentally acquired, —Cuba, Porto Rico and the Philippines—

with friendly, helping hands ; given Cuba to her own people ;_is perfectly willing to give the Philippines to their own people ; has educated rather than exploited, and has won friendship rather than enmity.   No nation, a few years ago, would ever have thought of doing anything other than seizing these lands and holding them forever, and *bleeding* them. If the United States, after preparing the Filipinos for self-government, will give them back their islands, and will promise to protect them from the greed of any other nation, she will have done the greatest act of national greatness history has known.

Furthermore, there are many evidences that this nation as a whole has no desire to seize any other nation's land but is conceiving for herself the part of peacemaker and general helper of the twenty republics south of her, which she has already drawn into a Pan-American union for their good.   Is it not true that the national ideals advanced by President Taft at the dedication of the palace presented by Mr. Carnegie to the Pan-American Union for its home, represent the growing convictions of the American people? The President said : " It goes without saying that in the foreign policy of the United States its greatest object is the preservation of peace among the American Republics." A year later, at the Third National Peace Congress at Baltimore, President Taft spoke in even stronger terms. He said: "The State Department at Washington has no more important or absorbing duty than to lend its good offices to the twenty republics of this hemisphere to prevent their various differences leading into war."

What ruler would have held up such things as ideals to his nation thirty years ago? If they really represent the ideals of our government, we are on the way to greatness. President Taft followed this remark with the statement that in his own administration this country, by using its kindly influence, had gone out of its way enough to prevent four wars among the republics. He also uttered these memorable words: "There is not, in the whole length and breadth of the United States, among its peoples, any desire for territorial aggrandizement, and its people, as a whole, will not permit this government, if it would, to take any steps in respect to foreign governments except those which will aid those foreign governments and those foreign people in maintaining their own government and in maintaining peace within their borders. . . . We have attained great prosperity and great power. We have become a powerful member of the community of nations in which we live, and there is, therefore, thrown upon us necessarily a care and responsibility for the peace of the world in our neighbourhood, and a burden of helping those nations that cannot help themselves."

Think of it! The President of the United States declaring to the world that this nation does not intend to steal any one's land and that her chief duty is *to help those nations that cannot help themselves!* Who ever heard of such a thing of a nation before! Of a man, yes—of all gentlemen. It is what makes men great. But of a nation, no. Yet we believe that the accomplishment of President Taft's high ideal is to be the nation's future claim for greatness. We believe that he echoed the thought of the people and we are glad. This country is on the way to greatness as thus she goes out to her sister republics.

But let us remember with much gratification that our nation has gone far beyond this hemisphere and rendered one service as far off as the Orient that was another one of these steps towards true greatness. After the Boxer Rebellion in China was quelled, the indemnity owing the United States was appraised at about $25,000,000. When about half of this amount had been paid, the United States government found that practically all losses had been covered and released China from paying the balance of the indemnity. The result is that China, after she got over the amazement such a deed on the part of a nation caused, sent a special envoy of high rank to Washington to thank our President and set aside the sum at home to send several hundred Chinese students to America every year. This is what came from "going out," rather than selfishly insisting on our whole pound of flesh.

It is but one instance of what should soon be happening continually. Soon the United States should be known throughout all the world as a nation whose sense of mission is as strong as that which dwelt in the breast of David Livingstone, whose greatness all the world has recently been celebrating. She should everywhere be designated as the nation whose friendliness was her highest attribute, and whose chief desire was the service of all peoples. Unconsciously she has already blessed many peoples. The South American republics caught their democratic impulse from her and made copious use of her constitution in framing their own.

Japan has studied her educational institutions, her commercial organization, her industrial methods, since the awakening of the East and sent thousands of her boys to America to learn of our best.

China is doing the same to-day. For many years now, our missionaries have been moulding the ideas as well as the ideals of all these nations, and most of the educational, philanthropic, medical, and technical methods now so rapidly spreading throughout Eastern nations were introduced by missionaries from America with their broad conception of the meaning of religion.

But now the time has come when *voluntarily*, and as her vocation and divine calling, the United States should enter upon the duty of going out, should assume the rôle of servant of the nations. The European powers are just now in a frenzy of alarm, a perfect nightmare of fears and jealousies that bids fair to plunge all Europe into a cataclysm that may almost wipe out its civilization.

Each nation is beginning to squeeze out the very life-blood of its people to pile up vast armaments on sea and land. As we write, Germany is asking the rich to sacrifice their fortunes for an army on a war footing. France is calling upon every man to throw up his

career and add one more year to the army.
Great Britain is piling up all the money she
can draw out of the people and putting it
into gunboats, while the people starve.   Ana-
tole France says it means the end of culture
in France, but everything must now go into
muskets and camps.   Germany's great industrial development must receive a check.
In Paris the students are again singing the
old war songs around the statue of Alsace
Lorraine.   It is all fraught with imminent
danger.   Nothing can stop it short of some
great machinery in which all the nations shall
have confidence, such as a permanent court
of arbitral justice and a concurrent agreement
of the nations to use it.

The United States should at once make
this her chief mission—to save these nations
from the sins which they would escape, but
seemingly, of their own motion, cannot.   She
should be willing for a while to turn some of
her self-directed energy to establishing this
permanent court of nations.   She should lift
up her voice without ceasing—day and night
demanding this permanent court and preach-
ing the substitution of judicial methods for
war in the settlement of all international disputes.   She should appoint a great committee of the leading peace workers and

statesmen of the nation to do nothing from to-day until the next Hague Conference but preach this thing. The Second Hague Conference, largely through the insistence of this government, voted in favour of such a Court, but many difficulties stood in the way of its speedy constitution.

The United States, in the face of the imperative call of the world, ought to engage all the best international lawyers of the world to work together in conference and be ready to attend the Third Hague Conference with a plan for a permanent court which will be approved by the nations. This nation ought at once, for the sake of the world, to offer every nation an absolute, unqualified treaty, agreeing to settle every kind of dispute by arbitration that individuals now settle by judicial methods. It might cost her something; she might be taking some risks, although she takes no more risk than does any man who passes self-defense over from pistols to courts. But all true greatness is willing to suffer some inconvenience for the larger good.

And should the United States lead in this thing, the blessing of the nations would be inevitable. All possibilities of wars with one great nation would be removed. The nations

of Europe and South America would soon begin to ask: "If this is possible between ourselves and the United States, why is it not
possible among ourselves?" Surely, such
treaties would follow. In time, as treaties
multiplied, the reasons for armaments would
disappear, and those fears of invasions and
outside attacks would slowly fade away.
Has not our nation the capacity to rise to
that point of greatness where every good
man easily and naturally stands, and make
this offer to the nations for the sake of their
salvation?

Shall she hesitate because of some little
risk? Why should not then every man who
forgets himself to some extent in serving his
neighbours or his country stop? Why
should not a nation be as ready to make
some sacrifices for the sake of the *world* as
a man is for the sake of the *nation?* Here
will be real national greatness when we reach
out towards this.

And finally, when the nations of the world,
looking to America, see that she is doing
some new thing among the nations: moving
along new ways, following some new impulse, concerning herself not with self-pro-
tection merely, putting stealing and oppression and exploitations of the weak as far be-

hind her as good men long ago put such things; forgetting herself sometimes and concerning herself chiefly with going out to do good; when the nations become confident, as soon they will, that the United States means nothing but good-will, justice, and friendliness to all peoples, then will she have accomplished more to bring universal peace than all active steps which she might take. For not only will she be immune from all danger, not only will she be able to offer mediation at any time of strain between other nations, not only will other nations seek her special friendship, but in the process of time they will see that *her way is the true way, the safe way* and *the right way*, and they too will begin to wonder if national greatness does not after all consist in those things which make *men* great: good-will, helpfulness, service, leadership into higher ways, going out.

## IX

## THAT NATION IS GREATEST WHICH FIRST PRACTISES REAL DEMOCRACY

SURELY the United States is great if democracy makes a nation great? No, for as yet she has not realized democracy. She has partially achieved it. To some degree her form of government is based upon it. The ideal is ever before her best citizens. She wears the name emblazoned upon her bosom. But real democracy has not yet been tried. If our nation can rise to it she shall be greatest of them all, and the light-bringer to the world. For all nations long for it, wait for it, and it is the ultimate political order of the world.

But as yet we are far off. In democracy the people rule, or at least choose those to whom they shall delegate that office. But in how many cities or states do the people actually rule, or say who shall rule? As this book was being written one man was calmly sitting in a restaurant in New York with a few henchmen about him picking out who should be the Democratic candidate for

Mayor of one of the biggest and greatest cities in the world. There are probably 350,000 Democrats in that city. Not twenty of them have had any say who should be nominated on the Democratic ticket. This same man largely controls the Legislature in the capital of his great state, and the legislators, instead of passing the laws the people want, pass those this great boss wants, even when these laws rob the people. This boss rule exists throughout the nation. It is in smallest villages, it is in all towns, it reaches its height of power in large cities. While it lasts there is no democracy. When the United States shall have rid herself of it, she will have taken one step towards greatness.

Two of the most incompatible things in the world are democracy and special privilege. Yet special privilege is continually being bought from our state legislatures and from the National Congress itself. Great corporations, railroads, industries, even societies are forever buying legislation—such legislation often robbing the people of millions of dollars. In how, many cities of the United 'States have not trolley companies, gas companies, all kinds of companies bought franchises that drained the people for generations? And who can believe that some tariff legislation, passed to protect some one special industry, has not sometimes been bought? Until this whole practise of buying and granting special legislation can be stopped, democracy has not come. And the test of national greatness will be democracy in the years before us.

Real democracy implies economic and social justice, as well as political. Economic justice implies the opportunity to work, just wages for work done, a fair share of the earnings produced, the certainty of food, shelter, and medical attendance to the end. We believe that hardly any one, with any love of humanity in him, any sense of the direction in which the world is moving, any prophetic instinct, will deny that this is a fair statement of *true* democracy. We are not here concerned with Socialism, Communism, Progressivism, or any other theory, movement or party.

We are not at all sure that the future political order will be any of which men now dream. It will combine some features of them all. It will be real democracy, whatever form it will assume, and it will provide justice for all. It will be more coöperative and less competitive. It will deal more with men as beings, and less with them as commodities, wage earners, economic units. It will consider their welfare as well as their capacity to earn. It will be fatherly in its attitude towards toilers, as well as businesslike. It will see that some provision is made for sickness, accident and old age, either by insurance, pensions or shares in the industry where one has worked. The government will exist for the welfare of all the people. Then democracy will have come.

To revert to a thought brought out in a previous chapter, true democracy will have a care of all its people, from the child to the tottering old man, and see, so far as in it lies, that each one gets opportunity, justice and happiness. It will see that all its children get proper education, that they are kept from too early work, and from work that dwarfs their development or sows seeds of ill health in their bodies. It will pay more attention to training its young men both how to get a living and how to live. It will devote itself to the health of the whole people. Nothing is more significant of the coming democracy of America than the growing movement *in the Government itself* to protect children, care for the national health, stop the manufacture and sale of poisonous foods and medicines.

It should be extended in many directions. It is all in the line of democracy. It will make us great.

No nation can be truly great nor have real democracy which has any vestige of race prejudice left in it, or which practises injustice to any class, or allows it to be practised within its borders. There can be no colour line, race line, language line, in democracy. Here is where democracy lingers in our own land. So long as we disfranchise a man because he is black, and not because he is incapable of intelligent participation in government, we are practising rank injustice, and democracy cannot survive injustice of any sort. So long as we socially ostracize a man because he happens to belong to a certain race, so long are we still unjust, that is, undemocratic. So long as we discriminate between classes on false and arbitrary distinctions, rather than on a basis of character, so long is democracy far from us. National greatness will come when every man in the nation receives *just* treatment, regardless of any outward mark.

There can never be a real democracy where idealism is absent from a people. Democracy cannot exist where material wealth is the only wealth of a nation. Indeed, the pursuit

of wealth alone develops just that spirit of
self which makes democracy impossible.
Democracy is based upon mutual coöperation, not "each for himself," but "each for
all." It is based on the desire to make one's
nation resplendent in the eyes of the world.
It is based on an idealism that puts the accomplishment of moral greatness above that
of vast fortunes, high buildings, long railroads, sumptuous palaces, multi-millionaires.
It is based, as we have seen, on justice. Let
not our material wealth swamp that idealism
on which democracy rests. Let us rise on
our wealth, more equally distributed as the
years go by, into the world of the spirit and
as a sun-crowned democracy be great.

Finally, democracy and militarism have no
part with each other, and cannot exist together. Democracy rests upon the wider
and wider diffusion of power among the people. Every additional soldier and every battle-ship means centralization of power in the
hands of, not the government only, but of the
man at the head of the government. It is
this militarism that makes democracy impossible in Russia. It is because democracy
is impossible in Germany so long as the gov
ernment has the vast army at its back tha*
the social democrats, the working men o₁

Germany are opposing militarism. It is because the working men of France see a blow
at democracy in the adding of an extra year
to the military service that they carried their
mile long petition against this act to the
Chamber of Deputies. It is this feeling that
the conscription and compulsory service in
the army which Lord Roberts and the Tories
are so frantically urging upon England is a
covert blow at democracy that it is being so
violently opposed. It behooves every American to watch very carefully every attempt to
militarize America, and see if it is not fear of
democracy that lies behind the movement
rather than fear of France and Germany.

There is a lurking suspicion in the minds
of those who are watching the struggle for
democracy in America that here, too, these
attempts to make militias part of the Regular
Army, increase the Army and Navy, to train
college boys to kill with precision, may be
more based on fear of the working men of
America by some capitalists and on the desire of some manufacturers of armament,
guns, nickel, and powder to amass vast fortunes and upon the desire to hold democracy
in check, more than upon patriotism or fear of
any outside enemies. However this may be
—and we believe it is true—every increase

in the Army and Navy of America means less power of the people, more power of the Government; less diffusion of government, more centralization of it; less democracy, more autocracy. But it is democracy that makes a nation great.

# X

## SOME INDICATIONS THAT THE UNITED STATES IS A GREAT NATION [1]

THE impression exists among many people that the United States became a world power when she conquered the Spaniards and sank a few worthless boats in Manila Harbour. There is no doubt that should the United States to-day go into Mexico and demolish the Mexicans and seize the land to be her own, one would

[1] In 1910 the author delivered an address "The United States and the Nations." In 1913, Edwin D. Mead, Secretary of the World's Peace Foundation, Boston, Mass., delivered a remarkable address in Chicago: "The United States as a World Power." As was inevitable, it covered much of the same ground as the author's address, and used some of the same illustrations. It has since been published in pamphlet form. In 1912 two striking books on Missions were published, both of which reveal on every page the wonderful part our nation has played in building Eastern civilizations; how she has been a world power since the first missionary landed in the East. These books are "Some By-Products of Missions," by Isaac Taylor Headland, Ph. D. (Eaton & Mains), and "Human Progress Through Missions," by James L. Barton, D. D. (Fleming H. Revell). This chapter is a review of these two books and Mr. Mead's address. The facts presented strikingly corroborate the contentions of the author in this book as to what makes a nation great.

hear vociferous talk in all directions about the United States again having manifested herself as a world power. As a matter of fact, the United States has been one of the greatest world powers continuously, since her birth in 1776. There has never been a year in all her history when she has not been exercising a most potent influence on the nations of the world, and the thing we most need to have impressed upon us in our day is that her influence through these years of peace has been infinitely greater than has ever come from any conquests she may have made by force. The influence which she exerted, for instance, in the Spanish War, is not to be named in the same breath with the influence which she has been continually exerting for a hundred years.

This has all been brought out so splendidly in a pamphlet by Edwin D. Mead, Secretary of the World's Peace Foundation, of Boston, that we cannot forbear giving in our last chapter a summary of his remarkable words. They are words which every man in the United States should read and ponder. Mr. Mead calls attention to the fact that there are two kinds of power in the world: moral power and physical power, or, in other words, the power of ideas and of materialism. In-

fluence which is exerted through moral power
and through ideas infinitely transcends any
influence which any nation exerts by force.
He then shows how true this has been of the
United States of America.   In the first part
of his pamphlet he dwells upon a theme on
which perhaps we have not sufficiently dwelt
in the United States, namely, the influence
of our country upon the motherland herself.
For Great Britain and all her colonies have
developed a good many of their political
institutions along lines in which the United
States has been pioneers.   Mr. Mead might
also have referred to the fact that that great
editor, William T. Stead, when he wrote his
book on the organization of the world, called
attention to the fact that the institutions which
should lie at the basis of this organization
would be patterned upon those in the United
States of America.   If we should have a
world court it would be patterned upon the
Supreme Court of the United States.   Were
we to have a world parliament, its organization would be largely based upon the Congress of the United States.   Mr. Mead dwelt
upon the fact that many of the colonies of
Great Britain, such colonies as Australia,
New Zealand and others, had almost literally
copied the political institutions of our coun-

try and based their constitutions upon them. Thus, the son has influenced the mother, and thoughtful Englishmen gratefully acknowledge this, and regret not that a hundred years ago we severed ourselves from direct relationships with them.

But Mr. Mead then proceeds to point out how this influence is making itself felt much more fully in many other parts of the world. How many realize that many of the leaders in the recent Balkan movement for national liberty and for freedom to develop along European rather than Asiatic lines were educated by American institutions? The best Bulgarians have received their training at Robert College, which was founded by Cyrus Hamlin, an American, and which has been run by American men and American money ever since. These young Bulgarian statesmen, even the Prime Minister, were educated at this little college at Constantinople. To quote a line from Mr. Mead: "So well was that known that when the great ships sailed away after the treaty of San Stefano, carrying the young men up through the Black Sea to their home to set up Bulgaria in self-government—as the great ships, I say, passed the little American college on the hill, every one dipped its flag, and every one with its great guns thundered its salute in reverent recognition of the American cradle of Bulgarian self-government. When we realize what has come from that, when we realize that out of Robert College there have been going, and are still going, young statesmen to make over Bulgaria, to make over Servia, to leaven Macedonia and to affect the whole Near East—we realize, then, something of the mighty influence of the United States as a world power through American ideas, something at this moment of concern to the Balkan States worth taking note of."

And at the same time the leaders of the Young Turks, those who have been standing for constitutional government in Turkey and those who would have saved their nation from the awful catastrophe which has descended upon her, and who would have had her keep her promises to the European nations and would have had her show tolerance in all her relations, were young men who have been educated at this same institution and owe their new-found vision of democracy to America, and to America alone.  Thus the United States through her schools and colleges is influencing all these Balkan Powers, and even Turkey herself, and whatever fine consummation may ultimately come out of this great struggle will be in some part due to the influence of the United states; an influence greater than any war or conquest she might ever have made.

In a most eloquent passage Mr. Mead calls attention to the influence of the United States in Japan. It was the United States which peacefully opened the doors of Japan to the new ideas, and which led her out of her former hermit condition, out of her isolation, into friendship and coöperation with the powers of the Western world. Ever since then the United States has exercised greater influence there than has any other nation. Not only has she sent her missionaries to Japan and established schools and colleges where the finest Japanese youth have been trained, but after they have been graduated from these local institutions they have almost invariably come to America and here studied our political and religious and commercial life, and gone back to become the leaders of their own country. Indeed, Japan has been so Americanized that often an American finds himself quite at home when he lands at Tokyo, so exactly are the Japanese institutions modelled on his own. One university alone, Doshisha, founded by

Americans, conducted for many years by a Japanese who was educated in America and by Americans, has turned out hundreds of Japanese boys and girls to be leaders of their nation ever since it was founded fifty years ago.   One fact to which Mr. Mead calls attention is that even the Japanese who came to this country to meet the Russians at the time of the settlement of the war had been educated in the United States.   And Mr. Mead then says: "When the president of the University of Kyoto, who was also the president of the Japanese Academy, was in this country three or four years ago he came to Boston, and I remember a speech of his at a dinner there.   The tribute paid by this eminent Japanese scholar to the United States and her influence upon Japan would have been something to give you pride in that kind of exercise of world power of which a country may indeed be proud.   And only two months ago we had in Boston Dr. Naruse, the head of the Japanese Women's College, in which a thousand women are studying.   Dr. Naruse, one who has himself felt the influences of American education, paid the highest tribute to American influences in the uplift of Japanese woman and in Japanese education altogether.   Why, the

basis of the agricultural college in Japan was
outlined by the first president of our agricultural college in Massachusetts."

In the same way Mr. Mead showed how
the United States had been a world power
in making the modern China. It is absolutely fair to say that no military power of
Europe, not even Germany or Great Britain,
has had anything like the shaping influence
upon the new China that the United States
has had, exercised absolutely in peaceful
ways and needing no power or force of any
kind behind it. Mr. Mead calls attention to
the fact that China contains one-fourth of the
population of the world, that she is going to
advance faster in the next fifty years than
Japan has advanced in the last fifty, and that
that advance will mean vastly more for the
world. In this advance, he says, the part
taken by the United States is most manifest.
All our relationships with China so far have
been on a most friendly basis. After the
Boxer revolution the indemnity which was
assessed by the United States was twenty-five
million dollars, but it was found that after all
bills had been paid, a half of that amount
still remained unused, and we never exacted
it from China. There was no return of
indemnity to China by any other nation, and

the impression made upon China was so great that she devoted that money to be used in sending five or six hundred students every year to America to study our institutions. These students are now going back to be leaders in China. All the new important positions in the government have been filled by these students. Talk about the influence of the United States ! What influence of any nation in the world backed by all the force at its command equals this influence which the United States is exercising upon China by a simple act of Christian good-will and friendship ? As Mr. Mead says : "More than one-half of the revolutionary Cabinet of Sun Yat Sen were men who had been educated in foreign universities, largely in American universities. A large proportion of the members of the present government of Yuan Shi-kai are men fitted in universities outside of China, largely American universities. The Chinese revolution has been a revolution of scholars, and those scholars got their inspiration and their self-governing ideas in high measure here in the universities of the United States. I was speaking at the University of Michigan in Ann Arbor, and I dined there with their Cosmopolitan Club. I learned to my surprise that there are in the University of Michigan sixty Chinese students—more in the University of Michigan than in any other single university—and several of those men are supported out of the indemnity fund. We have some of them in Massachusetts, at Harvard and elsewhere, and they are scattered all over the country. I wish that you knew these men as well as it has become my privilege and happiness to know them. Twice recently we have had a dozen or fifteen of them in our home; and could you talk with these young men, could you mark their beautiful spirit, their gentle manners, their high-mindedness, their thirst for knowledge, their public spirit, their ambition to serve China and carry over there all that is best in the United States, you would realize how immense the influence in the United States as a world power has been and may be in the making over of China. I say I know of nothing in human history more impressive, more momentous, than the fact that, at the same time, through the force in such high degree of American ideas, the Turkish tyranny should be thrust out of Europe and a federal republic be set up in China by men who profess as their highest ambition the establishment in China of a federal republic like the United States of America. My friends, beside this the talk of the United States becoming a world power because it sank half a dozen second rate Spanish gunboats a dozen years ago—why, my friends, that is so trivial, is such levity, that it makes serious and sober Americans blush with shame."

Mr. Mead might also have added that the whole new educational system of China is being based upon the educational system of the United States. She has sent many specialists here to study at first hand our methods, and she is even now bringing specialists from America to help her establish her school system. Her whole method of political preferment is being changed and is being based now upon capacity and upon merit and the new constitution of the government, as was the case with Japan, has been largely influenced by the political principles of our own land. (A Columbia University professor, Dr. Goodnow, has been called to China to advise in some changes in the Constitution.)

One frequently hears talk to the effect that while Germany is making ready by building her great navies, and Great Britain is all ready, to become world powers in their influence upon South America, that the United States, unless she equals them in

strength and force, cannot stand with them
as a great influence upon these southern
nations. People who think in this way should
read Mr. Mead's statements regarding our
influence in South America. Indeed, we are
practically the only nation who has ever had
any influence in South America, or who has
any to-day. Neither Germany nor Great
Britain bear any comparison with our nation
as a world power in South America. There
has not been a political constitution formed
by any nation to the south of us that has not
borne the impress of our own. Indeed, as
Mr. Mead intimates, it may fairly be said
that the impulse to democracy, the first reach-
ing out for a republican form of government
came after the United States had been made
a republic. The South American states
became republics because the United States
had made the system of government a success. They looked to us and followed in our
path. "Within a generation a whole continent made over through our exercise of
influence upon the institutions and constitutions of that continent! I think that is worth
recalling when men rise up and tell us that
we suddenly began to be a world power a
dozen years ago when we sank half a dozen
Second rate Spanish gunboats."

There were two books published in 1912
one, "Human Progress Through Missions,"
by Dr. James L. Barton, of the American
Board of Foreign Missions, of Boston ; another,
" Some By-Products of Missions," by Dr.
Isaac T. Headland, where again one sees
what a wonderful world power the United
States has been during the last hundred
years.   In these books one sees how the
colleges and churches and technical schools
and hospitals which the Americans have
founded in India, China, Japan, and Syria,
and in all parts of the world, for that matter,
have silently and quietly been transforming
the whole civilization of these lands.   They
have been centres of light.   From them have
flowed streams of influence which have grad-
ually and imperceptibly changed all sorts of
existing customs, and even modes of thought.
Altruism in India owes its origin to American
and British institutions ; it was an unknown
thing until the Western world came with its
gospel of service.   The hospitals and medical
schools and the colleges and the technical
schools in all of these countries have been
largely based upon the schools which the
missionaries have organized and conducted.
The new spirit of equality and the breaking
down of caste which is rapidly going on in

these lands had its origin largely because of contact with American homes which have been established by the missionaries throughout all these lands, and there is no doubt whatever that this whole spirit of democracy which is manifesting itself throughout the East can be traced almost directly back to our own land. And it is in these lines, not by military conquest, that the United States will always exercise the highest and greatest influence upon the other nations of the world. The greatest power is always exercised through kindly helpfulness, rather than through conquest.

If we knew of any one who was sceptical as to whether the United States could be a world power without a great navy, we would give him these two books. The *facts* are so given here that they are not only indisputable, but absolutely convincing. It is rather remarkable that two books covering practically the same ground should have come out so closely together. It only shows that two minds thoroughly conversant with the Eastern world have come to the same conclusions. This all carries weight, and perhaps it is a good thing that the books appeared together. Although they cover the same ground and show that practically everything

modern and worth while in the great Eastern
nations is a by-product of Christian missions,
yet each writer emphasizes things that particularly struck him in his studies, and thus
each book finely complements the other.
The two books differ a little, too, in their ap-
proach to the subject.  Dr. Barton deals in
more general terms with the permeation of
Eastern civilizations with Christian ideals.
Dr. Headland gives scores of illustrations
and concrete instances of the transformation
wrought in the communities where he has
lived, by the mere presence of the Gospel,
carried by American missionaries.  Dr.
Headland also fortifies his claims that the
East cannot come to greatness without the
Gospel, by appealing to history.  He shows
that the nations of to-day, which have the
political power of the world, the trade, the
science, the great industries, the inventions,
the universities, are the nations where the
Bible has been an open book and the Gospel
freely preached.  History is simply repeat-
ing itself in the Orient.  Both books show
how practically the whole market for Western commodities has followed our missionaries.  It is much truer to say that " Trade
follows the mission " than "Trade follows
the flag."  Thus attention is called to the

fact that the first Singer sewing machine to enter China was carried by an American missionary. The Chinese saw it and wanted it. The same is true of agricultural implements and industrial machinery. The simple fact is that those Eastern nations which have any science, any industry, any commerce or any healing, got them from America, and they were not in India, China, or Japan until we went there. They are common everywhere in those countries now.

Here are some of the great by-products of missions, some facts of human progress through missions, dwelt upon by these books : There was no healing in the Eastern nations until the Gospel came. Hospitals were unheard of and the suffering was fearful. The so-called physicians made it worse. If a man got a fish bone in his throat incantations were used. These books give most pitiable and amusing incidents of attempts at surgery. But the Christian doctor came with the missions, and generally from America. He healed many. But the *by-product* is the great thing. China and Japan began establishing medical schools with missionaries at their head. Now medical schools and hospitals are being built all over the Eastern nations, modelled upon American institutions.

The same has been true of the educational system of the East.   The whole university, college, and school system of the Eastern nations is largely a result of the schools our missionaries established, and, as we saw in the case of China, these governments have generally called upon our missionaries to be organizers and presidents and teachers, until a native force could be trained.   All over the East fine technical schools are being established.   They mean a new civilization soon to follow.   But technical schools were never heard of until our missionaries came.   Both of these books show how democracy has been a by-product of missions.   The foundation-stone on which all democracy rests is the worth and potential capacity of man.   There is little sense of this in non-Christian lands. It lies inherent in every word of Jesus Christ. You cannot even drop a New Testament into China or India without starting a ferment. The Gospel always precedes a revolution. The republic of China is a by-product of the Gospel carried by American missionaries, who have put the book into everybody's hands.   Again, Eastern religions are not big enough for republican forms of government. They cannot meet the new national requirements.   As a result, republicanism, created by the ferment of the Gospel in men's minds, is now reacting in favour of Christianity, a religion big enough for democracy. Christianity alone provides adequate motive and power for modern life.

Both of these books are explicit in their story of the change in the home life of the East, caused simply by each town and city *seeing* a Christian home. The home has been copied. Says Dr. Barton: "The external conditions of the Eastern home have met with marked change. It is impossible that the same relations shall continue to exist between the educated and intelligent wife and her husband that formerly prevailed between the husband and his ignorant and untutored wife. Rapidly the wife's position is rising from that of a servant or a toy to that of a companion or associate, possessing a common interest with her husband, and capable of contributing to the intellectual, moral, and social equipment of the home. . . . Simultaneously there has come an endeavour to make more beautiful, wholesome and sanitary the externals of the home itself."

Dr. Headland shows the influence of our missions upon the sanitary conditions of the East in this striking paragraph: "Every few years there breaks out in these filthy Oriental cities a plague which strikes terror to the hearts, not only of the people among whom it starts, but in the hearts of those also at the remotest ends of the earth.   Cholera, bubonic and pneumonic plague, dengue, berberi, and others.   Do we ever ask ourselves why all these plagues take their rise in Asia?   And do we try to answer that why?   One word tells the tale: it is dirt.   Nay, a better word is filth; for dirt does not express the filthiness of Asiatic dirt.   It cannot be expressed in the English language; for the English language, since it has been a language, has never lived long among such *Tsang*.   That is the word that expresses it—*Tsang*.   There is but one remedy for this dirt, and that remedy is the Gospel.   Wherever the Gospel has gone, cleanliness has gone, and up to the present the world has never produced a clean city where the influences of the Gospel have not gone.   If I did not believe in foreign missions for any religious reasons, I would believe in them and support them for the sanitary influence they have had upon the world.   A member of a great bathtub manufacturing firm told me at the Duquesne Club in Pittsburgh recently that since the missionaries have gone to China, they are shipping thousands of bathtubs to that great empire."

So these books go on, convincingly revealing the by-products of our missions, the human progress, in civics, art, morals, manner, social life, humaneness, ideals—in every department of life, in every relation. Especially, as comprehending them all, above the direct results of the Gospel in converting human hearts to the serviceful life, a new spirit of life is coming over all nations, namely, the altruistic, serviceful spirit, absolutely unknown before the Gospel came. Says Dr. Barton : "When a missionary in Africa suggested to some natives that a much used public trail should be constructed, they replied, 'Never since the Zambesi ran into the sea was such a thing dreamed of as that we should make a road for other people to walk on.' That is the idea that has held Africa and Asia for centuries in the grip of selfish and narrow-minded individualism." Care for the weak, the sick, the crippled, the poor, was unknown. The idea of a rich, strong, educated man giving his life to elevate the poor, the weak and the ignorant had no force in the East. But now one will find it everywhere, especially in Japan. Through our missions, our schools, our hospitals, our books, our ideals, our statesmen, our inventions, our political institutions copied, we

**120  Indications that the United States**

have been perhaps the greatest world power since Palestine, Rome and Greece. Not by might, but by our service, have we conquered the nations.

*FREDERICK LYNCH, D. D.*

# The New Opportunities of the Ministry

With Introduction by Hugh Black, M.A., D.D.
12mo, cloth, net 75c.

The ringing, positive message which this book bears is most opportune. It is written by a man who fully appreciates the significance of the pastoral vocation and has the genius to put his conception into trenchant, stirring phrases. That the highest opportunities in life are to-day open to the pastor are conclusively and triumphantly shown.

*NEWELL DWIGHT HILLIS, D.D.*

# All the Year Round

An Outlook upon its Great Days. 12mo, cloth, net $1.20.

Dr. Hillis' characteristics as a preacher are so well known that it is hardly necessary to point out that this volume of "Sermons for Occasions" is distinguished by originality of thought, felicitous illustrations and distinction of style. Here the reader will find material for each great festival day of the church, and each national holiday, that will give deeper meaning to the "days we celebrate."

*RUSSELL H. CONWELL, D. D.*

# How to Live the Christ Life

12mo, cloth, net $1.00.

Doctor Conwell is a master of the art of presenting and enforcing truth with dramatic, unusual, gripping narratives. This selection of some of his best sermons well illustrates his genius. These discourses should serve the double purpose of stimulating Christian readers to renewed endeavor to reach a higher level of living and to winning those who have not begun to live the Christ life.

*W. L. WATKINSON, D. D.*

# Life's Unexpected Issues

and Other Papers on Character and Conduct.
12mo, cloth, net $1.00.

"A book of seventeen addresses on character and conduct, all of which are fresh and fine in thought, style, and spirit. To those who have heard or read after Doctor Watkinson, no word of commendation need be spoken of these splendid papers, the first of which gives title to the volume. The table of contents is most inviting, and each topic is taught and interpreted in a simple, helpful way."—*Religious Telescope.*

*REV. WILFRED S. HACKETT*

# The Land of Your Sojournings

12mo, cloth, net $1.00.

"To pastors and laymen who find themselves submerged in the dispiritualizing atmosphere of our daily life, this true spiritual philosopher speaks with wise, mellow, tender counsel. His style is luminous, expository and fraught with a wealth of illustrations."—*Twentieth Century Pastor.*

**HUGH BLACK, M.A.**          *Author of "Friendship," etc.*

## Happiness

Pocket Edition. *Uniform with "Work."* 16mo, cloth, gilt top, net $1.00.

"Only those who are constitutionally pessimistic and temperamentally incapable of optimism cannot fail to find here something good. A book like this now and then is needed. The calm beauty of the author's style soothes and makes for peace, and peace is the heart of happiness."—*Minneapolis Journal.*

**JOHN HENRY JOWETT, D.D.**

## Things That Matter Most

Devotional papers. 12mo, net $1.25.

Brief devotional messages of the great preacher possessing the simplicity, the earnestness and directness which have made Dr. Jowett unfailingly helpful. Those who have come to look to him for spiritual uplift and comfort will find him here at his best.

**MALCOLM JAMES McLEOD, D.D.**

## Letters to Edward

12mo, cloth, net $1.00.

The letters which make up this volume let the reader into the heart life of one of America's most popular preachers. Dr. McLeod has visualized the present day world in which a metropolitan pastor moves, in a delightfully realistic way. His letters are human and appealing.

**JOHN DOUGLAS ADAM, D.D.**

## Letters of Father and Son During a College Course          12mo, cloth, net $1.00.

"If some one financially able would determine that a free copy of this book should go into every home, from which students will go, our colleges would take on new life. Every phase of a student's needs is discussed with a sanity and winsomeness that will make every old student feel that such a book in his hands, during his college days, would have furnished an inspiration."—*Heidelberg Teacher.*

**JOHN T. FARIS, D.D.**

## Seeking Success

A Companion to "Making Good." 8vo, net $1.25.

In this new volume Mr. Faris fully maintains the reputation he has gained as a writer of inspirational literature for boys and young men. These glimpses of actual events in the lives of boys and men can hardly fail to play an important part in forming right ideals in the minds of the readers.

# ESSAYS, GIFT BOOKS, ETC.

## NEWELL DWIGHT HILLIS, D.D.

### Lectures and Orations by Henry Ward Beecher

Collected and with Introduction by Newell Dwight Hillis. 12mo, cloth, net $1.20.

It is fitting that one who is noted for the grace, finish and eloquence of his own addresses should choose those of his predecessor which he deems worthy to be preserved, the most characteristic and the most dynamic utterances of America's greatest pulpit orator.

## DAVID SWING

### The Message of David Swing to His Generation Addresses and Papers, together with a Study of David Swing and His Message by Newell D. Hillis

12mo, cloth, net $1.20.

A collection of some of David Swing's greatest orations and addresses, mostly patriotic, none of which have before been published in book form. Dr. Hillis, who has gathered them together, contributes an eloquent tribute to his distinguished confrere in an Introductory "Memorial Address."

## WAYNE WHIPPLE

### The Story-Life of the Son of Man

8vo, illustrated, net $2.50.

Nearly a thousand stories from sacred and secular sources woven into a continuous and complete chronicle of the life of the Saviour. Story by story, the author has built up from the best that has been written, mosaic like, a vivid and attractive narrative of the life of lives. Mr. Whipple's life stories of Washington and Lincoln in the same unique form, have both been conspicuously successful books.

## GAIUS GLENN ATKINS, D. D.

### Pilgrims of the Lonely Road

12mo, cloth, net $1.50.

In nine chapters the author presents what he calls the "Great Books of the Spirit". Beginning with the Meditations of Marcus Aurelius, he interprets with spiritual insight and clarity of expression the Confessions of St. Augustine, Thomas a'Kempis' Imitation of Christ, the Theologia Germanica, Bunyan's Pilgrim's Progress, etc.

## ROSE PORTER

### A Gift of Love and Loving Greetings for 365 Days

*New Popular Edition.* Long 16mo, net 50c.

"All the texts chosen present some expressions of God's love to man, and this indicates the significance of the title."
—*The Lutheran Observer.*

CLARA E. LAUGHLIN *Author of "Everybody's Lonesome"*

## The Work-A-Day Girl

A Study of Present Day Conditions. Illustrated, 12mo, cloth, net $1.50.

Few writers to-day have given more serious and sympathetic consideration to the difficulties which beset the American working girl. The book is frank and outspoken, but not too much so for there is need of plain talk on a matter so vital to our social welfare.

FREDERIC J. HASKIN *Author of "The American Government"*

## The Immigrant: An Asset and a Liability

12mo, cloth, net $1.25.

"Persons are asking how they may best do their duty and their whole duty to those coming to our shores. This book is a valuable light on the subject. It is full of facts and it is a capable and conscientious study as to the meaning of the facts. Any thoughtful person will find here much valuable material for study and the book is calculated to do much good."—*Herald and Presbyter.*

CHARLES STELZLE

## The Gospel of Labor

12mo, cloth, net 50c.

"Sometimes it is a short sermonette, sometimes it is a story, but every one of the thirty-three chapters is a presentation in terse, graphic English of some phase of the gospel of labor by a man who knows the life of labor from the inside. A stimulating message for the laboring man, and many valuable suggestions for those who desire to enter into his life in the most helpful way."—*Presbyterian Advance.*

PROFESSOR JAMES R. HOWERTON

## The Church and Social Reform

12mo, cloth, net 75c.

"In a succinct and yet very thorough manner the author discusses the fundamentals of this present-day problem of the relation of the church to social reform, and the obligations entailed. The volume is an exceptionally helpful one, serving to clear the atmosphere and show the way out."—*Christian World.*

P. MARION SIMMS

## What Must the Church Do to Be Saved?

The Necessity and Possibility of the Unity of Protestantism. 12mo, cloth, net $1.50.

From a first-hand observation the author brings together a body of facts which emphasize strongly the necessity for a practical union among the denominations of the Church of Christ in America to fulfill her mission. The remedies proposed by the author are set forth with a reasonableness and straightforwardness which invite the respect of all readers.

*HENRY C. McCOMAS, Ph.D.*

## The Psychology of Religious Sects

**A Comparison of Religious Types. Cloth, net $1.25.**

A study of the origin of the various denominations. When and how did they begin? Is there real need for one hundred and eigthy odd sects in America or are they a positive hindrance to the Church? The scientific spirit is in evidence throughout these chapters but so, also is the spirit of reverence. The book is constructive not iconoclastic.

*CHARLES STELZLE*

## American Social and Religious Conditions

**Illustrated with numerous charts and tables. 12mo, cloth, net**

This work may be used both as a text book for study classes and for general reading. It contains the findings of the Men and Religion Surveys in seventy principal cities, of which the author had charge. Mr. Stelzle also served as the dean of the Social Service throughout the Movement. Out of a wide and practical experience in City Work the author discusses a program for the Church, especially with regard to the "down-town" situation. The book contains many original charts and diagrams.

*CHARLES S. MACFARLAND*

## Spiritual Culture and Social Service

**12mo, cloth, net $1.00.**

A stirring call to service. Dr. Macfarland, as pastor of Congregational churches in large industrial centres, has had first hand experience in some of the most pressing problems now confronting the church. As secretary of the Social Service Commission of the Council of Churches of Christ in America, he is now engaged in solving the problem in a larger way. He has a message to deliver and he presents it with a force and conviction that cannot fail to deeply impress and influence the reader.

*ARTHUR V. BABBS, A.B.*

## The Law of the Tithe

**As Set Forth in the Old Testament. 12mo, cloth, net $1.50.**

"A book of very genuine scholarship—a complete history of the universality of the tithe—the ablest and perhaps the most interesting explanation of this ancient custom that has appeared."—*N. Y. Christian Advocate.*